The Best of *NOTES Plus*

W9-BJO-541

Selected by
Ruth Cline

National Council of Teachers of English
1111 Kenyon Road, Urbana, Illinois 61801

Staff Editor: Felice A. Kaufmann

Cover Design: Michael Getz

Book Design: Tom Kovacs for TGK Design

Illustrators: Louise Krauss; Richard Maul

NCTE Stock Number 33657

It is the policy of NCTE in its journals and other publications to provide a forum for the open discussion of ideas concerning the content and the teaching of English and the language arts. Publicity accorded to any particular point of view does not imply endorsement by the Executive Committee, the Board of Directors, or the membership at large, except in announcements of policy, where such endorsement is clearly specified.

Library of Congress Cataloging-in-Publication Data

The Best of Notes plus / selected by Ruth Cline.
    p.   cm.
    Reprint. Originally published: Urbana, Ill. : National Council of
Teachers of English. c1989.
    ISBN 0-8141-3365-7
    1. Language arts (Secondary)—United States. I. Cline, Ruth K.
J. II. Notes plus.
LB1631.B43   1991
428'.0071'2—dc20   90-47670
                                                                CIP

Contents

Preface

Since *NOTES Plus* began publication in September 1983, readers have expressed special appreciation for the feature columns "Classic of the Month," "Literature Assignment of the Month," and "Writing Assignment of the Month." The format of these three columns allows teachers to share longer and more involved strategies for enhancing the study of literature and writing. In this volume are collected some of the best of those activities and lesson plans. If you find them useful in your teaching of literature and writing, you might consider returning the favor and sharing your own classroom ideas with other teachers through *NOTES Plus*. (Submissions to *NOTES Plus* may be sent to *NOTES Plus*, NCTE, 1111 Kenyon Road, Urbana, IL 61801.)

Classic of the Month

Our Town

Thornton Wilder's *Our Town* should be on every American's reading list. The possessive pronoun tells us why—it's ours. It belongs to all of us. As the hymn ("Blest Be the Tie That Binds") repeated in the play suggests, the play itself links us to the very center of ourselves—and to the universe. Similarly, the address on Jane Crofut's envelope tells us that she is an ordinary person living in a microscopic spot in the universe, yet she contains, as do we all, an entire universe. Wilder's play leads us not only into the center of our selfhood but outward to family, friends, and strangers throughout time and space. *Our Town* binds us to one another in joy, in love, and in reverence at the same time that we recognize the pain of loss, the sorrow of ignorance, and the regrets for weakness.

Questions about Form

1. How is reading a play different from reading other forms of literature? What special demands does this play make upon its readers or audience?

2. Discuss characteristics of this play that distinguish it from other plays: minimal set, actors among the audience, simultaneous actions, the role of the Stage Manager, the role of the audience. What is the impact of these special effects?

3. Discuss the title of the play as well as its three-part structure: Daily Life, Love and Marriage, and Death. Comment, too, on the dates of each act.

4. We think of plays and novels as having a hero or heroine. Who is the hero or heroine of *Our Town*? How do you know?

5. Why does Wilder use two families so similar in makeup as the focus of the action? Why is one father the town doctor and the other the

editor of the local newspaper? List the minor characters and decide what their functions are.

Interpreting the Play

1. In his opening lines, the Stage Manager says, "In our town we like to know the facts about everybody." What other references to facts can you find? What do the facts reveal? What do they fail to reveal?

2. Who *is* the Stage Manager? Look through the play and jot down whatever seems to be a clue. Come to a conclusion that you can defend with specific evidence.

3. Even though George's father is a college graduate, he doesn't pressure George to go to college. Should he have? Find a copy of John Updike's poem "Ex-Basketball Player." Compare it with what Wilder seems to be saying about staying in our own backyards.

4. Rituals play a part in the action of the play, just as rituals play a part in our lives. What formal and informal rituals are enacted or referred to in the play? What are they meant to suggest?

5. Discuss the relationships between adults and children, and between parents and children in the play. Compare them with those types of relationships today.

Planning Small Group Activities

1. Divide the class into six groups and assign two groups to each of the three acts. Ask each group to make two lists based on their assigned acts—one of details that seem dated and the other of details that seem to apply to their lives now. Later, arrange for the two groups assigned to the same act to meet together and compare lists, resolve discrepancies, summarize findings, and write conclusions. One representative for each act then reports the conclusions to the class. What insights are gained?

2. Students in small groups select a scene of their choice and rewrite it, placing it in a different time frame. Later, they act out the new scene for the class. After the presentation, the class discusses the effect of the time change.

3. A group of students might enjoy looking through Edgar Lee Masters' *Spoon River Anthology* and staging a dramatic reading of

the lines of selected characters. Follow with a class discussion that compares Masters' work with the third act of *Our Town.*

4. Ask students to form a panel that will investigate the attitudes towards small towns expressed by other writers—Hamlin Garland and Sinclair Lewis, for example.

5. Encourage students interested in photography or film to put together a slide/tape presentation that conveys the essence of Our Town, 1984.

Writing Assignments about the Play (Directions to Students)

1. Explore in an essay what Wilder seems to be saying about life and death. Document your conclusions with specific details from the play; for example, in the last act Emily asks, "Live people don't understand, do they?"

2. Since Mr. Webb is editor of the newspaper, he will write his daughter's obituary. Put yourself in his place and write that obituary.

3. Write a description of George and Emily's wedding for the society column or a sports feature on George's high school career in baseball.

4. Write an essay related to the incident when George's father rewards his son for neglecting to chop the wood. Comment on his use of psychology and his theory of discipline.

5. Gossip plays a role in Wilder's play. Find those speeches that seem to be gossip, analyze what is being said, and write an essay drawing conclusions about the positive and negative effects of gossip, being

sure to use references to speeches you've pulled from the play as well as from real life.

Beverly Haley, The Language Works, Fort Morgan, Colorado

The Great Gatsby

Fast cars, wild parties, shady business dealings. . . . These are a few of the intriguing elements found in F. Scott Fitzgerald's *The Great Gatsby*— a novel that invites its readers to enter the Jazz Age. Studying *The Great Gatsby* promotes discussion of values; the glittering world of the Roaring Twenties appeals to students, yet at the same time they are able to detect the artificiality and moral bankruptcy of the society Fitzgerald depicts. Obtain if you can the film version of *The Great Gatsby* starring Robert Redford and Mia Farrow; it paints a memorable portrait of the excessive opulence of Gatsby's world.

In addition to presenting provocative subject matter, *The Great Gatsby* teaches important stylistic lessons. Through Nick Carraway, it provides an excellent example of a first-person retrospective point of view. Students can learn the technical demands an author faces in using a central intelligence. They can also learn how effective this point of view is for charting the growth in the insight of a narrating character. A second stylistic feature is the use of a complex chronology, one that shifts back and forth between the present and the past. This type of chronology provides a complete picture of the protagonist only at the end of the work, and is typical of modern literature. Yet a third lesson stems from the use of imagery clusters. Because of the brevity of the novel, students can easily trace the patterns of images that Fitzgerald emphasizes.

Class Discussion

There's nothing like a good discussion question to inspire creative dispute among members of the class. Here are questions that you can use along with your own favorites, either during the course of reading the novel or after everyone in the class has finished reading.

1. What is the significance of the title *The Great Gatsby?* Is Jay Gatsby truly great? Explain your answer.

2. How is marriage depicted in the novel? How successful is the marriage between Daisy and Tom Buchanan? And that between Myrtle and George Wilson?

3.   What is Gatsby's dream? Does he ever see Daisy as she really is?

4.   Compare Jay Gatsby to James Gatz. What does Fitzgerald mean when he writes that "Jay Gatsby of West Egg, Long Island, sprang from his Platonic conception of himself"?

5.   How does Fitzgerald reveal that Gatsby is an isolated character?

6.   What does the novel say about materialism? What, if any, are the similarities between the 1920s and the 1980s?

7.   How does Fitzgerald relate Gatsby's dream to the American Dream? What seems to be his message about the American Dream as expressed in the last two paragraphs of the novel?

Writing Assignments

As a follow-up to reading and discussion, suggest one of the writing assignments listed below.

1.   Look up the word *hedonism* in the dictionary and write a short essay revealing how the concept applies to Fitzgerald's novel.

2.   Compose a paragraph on each of the following items, explaining how each reflects Gatsby's tastes and lifestyle:
   a.   his house
   b.   his car
   c.   his parties
   d.   his guest list (given in Chapter IV)

3.   Pretend that you are Nick Carraway and write two journal entries, one giving your impression of Jay Gatsby upon first meeting him and the other giving your final assessment of the man after you've returned to the Midwest.

4.   Compare Tom Buchanan's relationship with his wife, Daisy, to his relationship with Myrtle Wilson. What does he want from each woman? Does he love either of them?

5.   Some critics suggest that although Gatsby is the principal figure in the action of the novel, Nick is the most significant character. Discuss the novel as a record of Nick's moral development. What does Nick learn from his experiences in the East?

Small Group Activities

Here are some additional ideas you might try when teaching *The Great Gatsby*.

1. Divide the class into research teams and ask them to provide the class with information about the Roaring Twenties. Give each group a list of one or more questions such as the following:

   a. What was the political climate of the United States during the decade? Who were the country's major political leaders? How did people respond to the aftermath of World War I?

   b. What was the economic status of the United States? Was the decade a time of growth or recession? Explain why.

   c. What was Prohibition and how did it affect the nation?

   d. What was the status of women at this time? What changes were occurring in the institution of marriage and in young people's moral standards?

   e. What types of music were popular? What subjects were mentioned in popular song lyrics? Do you think that young people in the 1920s listened to popular music for the same reasons that young people today do? If so, what are those reasons?

2. Assign one major character—Jay Gatsby, Nick Carraway, Daisy Buchanan, Tom Buchanan, and Jordan Baker—to each of five groups. Ask each group to decide upon three adjectives that best describe the character and to be able to explain the reasons for selecting these words. Have each group select one passage from the novel that seems to reflect the character's personality well.

3. Form teams of students to examine the imagery in the novel. Each team must search for one particular set of images that recur throughout the novel. Among the possibilities are the following images:

   a. color (especially green)

   b. eyes or vision (whether accurate or distorted)

   c. a wasteland (a barren landscape, ashes, dust)

   d. cars

   e. time

   f. death

4. Appoint a group of students to trace the novel's chronology. The group should consider these questions: In what season does the book begin? In what season does Nick first go east? In what season does Gatsby die? In what chapter(s) do we learn of Gatsby's boyhood? Of his adolescence? Of his early business dealings?

5. Divide the class into three groups and assign each group to prepare a brief talk, based on passages from the book, on one of the following topics:

   a. Nick's role *as narrator*, including where he is when he is writing the book, what his attitude toward Jay Gatsby is, and how he solves the problem of presenting information that he did not witness.

   b. Nick *as a man* who gets caught up in the corrupt world of the East. Decide if and when Nick seems not to act according to his moral standards.

   c. Nick *as a detached character*. In what ways is he involved in the action and in what ways is he separate from it?

Lynn P. Shackelford, Greenville, South Carolina

To Kill a Mockingbird

Harper Lee's Pulitzer Prize novel *To Kill a Mockingbird* (1960) captivates readers of all ages. It's a story that can be read on several levels, a story whose characters teach us to be aware of the dark parts of ourselves we want to bury and remind us as well to pay homage to our nobler qualities.

The book's title, coupled with periodic references in the novel to the mockingbird, points out the theme. This theme is activated by Atticus's repeated admonitions to his children to look at the world from the other person's point of view—to develop and practice compassion toward others. The title hints, too, of the sadness we should feel toward any person who has never learned—or been allowed to learn—to sing his or her own song.

If you decide to use the novel for class study, plan to adapt the following discussion topics, activities, and writing assignments to the abilities and interest levels of your group.

Suggested Discussion Topics

1. Consider the title of the novel and how it captures the primary theme. Find all the instances in the book that refer to killing a mockingbird and discuss how each situation illuminates the theme.

2. Analyze the form of the novel from several aspects: 1) its division
    into two parts—what happens in each part and what is the purpose
    for the division; 2) the novel's double narrator—the grown-up Jean
    Louise sometimes superimposed and sometimes separate from the
    child Scout—and the effects achieved by this technique; 3) the
    episodic nature of the main story, setting into relief the courtroom
    drama.

3. Discuss the fact that Aunt Alexandra insists Jean Louise know the
    details of her background. What does this reveal about Alexandra
    and about the times in which she lived? Are attitudes today in this
    regard similar to or different from those depicted in the novel? In
    what ways does living in her brother's house change Alexandra and
    how does her presence change Scout?

4. Discuss the symbolism of the "mad dog" episode in Chapter 10.
    Discuss, too, how the chapter foreshadows future events and chan-
    ges the way the children view their father.

5. Discuss what Miss Maudie tells Scout and Jem about the fact that
    their father is one of those rare people who carry out painful tasks
    on behalf of us all. What people (generally and specifically) are
    doing this kind of work for us today?

6. At the end of Chapter 25 we read: "Atticus had used every tool
    available to free men to save Tom Robinson, but in the secret courts
    of men's hearts Atticus had no case." Analyze what is meant by "the
    secret courts of men's hearts." Draw parallels to similar situations
    today.

7. Analyze the concept of winning and losing according to Jem's view
    of the jury's verdict and then according to Atticus's view. Draw
    conclusions that can be applied to any winning and losing situation.

Large Group Activities

1. View the film version of the novel. Compare and contrast the film
    and the book and discuss the overall effects of each on the viewer
    or reader.

2. Consider the trial:
    a. Those who are interested might research the court systems
        under different governments, analyzing the system and the

language of that system compared to the language used in the text.

   b. Analyze the effect that the composition of the jury had on the verdict.

3. Consider the theme of the "outsider:"

   a. List the number of characters who are "outsiders" in the novel, along with a brief statement explaining what conditions make each an outsider.

   b. List people who (generally or specifically) are considered "outsiders" within the nation, your community, and your school. Think of times you've felt like an outsider and explain what made you feel left out. Or think of instances in which you or a group to which you belonged made someone else an outsider; explain the circumstances.

   c. Read other books that use the "outsider" or minorities as their theme. Briefly report to the class on how the theme is dramatized; then, as a group, draw parallels among all the readings and offer your opinions as to whether this situation can ever be remedied. If so, how? If not, why? How can one best cope with being an outsider?

Small Group or Individual Activities

1. Create a book cover design for the novel, or make a series of sketches illustrating each example of Atticus's admonitions to the children to "stand in the other person's shoes."

2. Dramatize a scene from the novel. Scenes to consider might be Scout's first day at school, the women's missionary group meeting, or the scene on Halloween night when Bob Ewell is murdered.

3. Make an illustrated map showing the town and marking the special locations referred to in the novel.

4. Form a small group and choose one of the following topics. Discuss your topic, draw conclusions, and share your opinions with the class.

   a. The relationships between parents and children (the Radleys, the Finches, the Cunninghams, the Ewells, the Robinsons, and Dill's family).

   b. Churches and religion in the town of Maycomb.

   c. The class system of Maycomb and what it shows about values and beliefs.

   d. The effects of poverty and ignorance on individuals and on the community of Maycomb.

   e. A quotation from the story that you find meaningful and significant in relation to the rest of the novel.

Writing Assignments

1. Expository

   a. Write a book of etiquette according to the rules of Maycomb society.

   b. Trace the character development of either Jem or Scout throughout the novel, charting the steps each takes toward adulthood.

   c. In Chapter 22, Atticus comments that when injustices occur (such as Tom's being condemned), it "seems that only children weep." Explain his observation in light of the novel's story and themes.

   d. Explain how setting becomes an important element in the novel, using specific examples from the text.

2. Choose a Creative Writing Assignment

   a. Write journal entries, a letter, or a poem from the point of view of *one* of the following characters: Tom Robinson, his wife, Boo Radley, Mayella Ewell, Mrs. Dubose.

   b. Write a humorous essay, narrative, or verse on "being a lady" from Scout's point of view.

   c. Write a "Dear Abby" letter and response that fit a situation in the novel; for example, advice to Aunt Alexandra on how to manage Scout, or advice to Scout on how to get along with the now-teenaged Jem.

Beverly Haley, The Language Works, Fort Morgan, Colorado

Julius Caesar: **To Teach or Not to Teach**

Teaching *Julius Caesar* to sophomores can prove to be an arduous task. Students usually greet the subject of Shakespeare with disdain and are hard to convince of the value of keeping an open mind. To boost student interest in our study of *Julius Caesar,* I rely on supplementary activities that make use of library, speaking, and writing skills.

1. Transforming the classroom into "downtown Rome" not only creates the right atmosphere for studying *Julius Caesar,* but promotes student involvement. Students cover the classroom walls with travel posters, maps, pictures, and anything else that seems appropriate, using as sources travel agencies, encyclopedias, atlases, and library books. Students can also paint their own travel posters and maps on roll paper and can create advertisements for goods, services, or forms of entertainment that might have been available in ancient Rome.

2. An eyewitness news team can provide an exciting vantage point from which to view the events in the play. A news team consisting of an anchorperson, a sportscaster, and a weather forecaster is selected by random drawing or by the appointment of volunteers at the beginning of each new act of the play. The members of the news team work together to create short news stories based on the previous day's reading, to write short editorials or commentaries, and to write reports on sports and weather using information gathered from the encyclopedia and library books. At the beginning of each class period, the current news team gives a ten-minute presentation.

    To help students transform an event from the play into the format of a news story, you may want to provide copies of a form like this one:

    Format for News Copy

    Reporter:

    Who was involved?

    What happened?

    When did it happen?

    Where did it happen?

    Why did the situation occur?

    What were the results of the situation?

    Quote(s) from person interviewed:

    Reporter's opinion on event:

Suggest that members of the news team spend ten or fifteen minutes talking together about that day's reading and the ensuing discussion. As they plan the next day's news stories, encourage them to divide up the writing so that students work on more than one type of story while on the news team.

3. To focus on important characters and events in the play, have student groups explicate significant quotations and present their insights to the class. Prepare a list of quotations from the text you are using or use the list I've prepared. Divide students into several groups and distribute a different list of five or six quotations to each group. (I divide students into three groups by handing out lollipops of three different colors as students enter the classroom and by asking students to group themselves according to the color of their lollipops. This tactic may not have a lot to do with *Julius Caesar,* but it seems to start the class period out on a good note.)

Each group is to identify the speaker, audience, situation, and overall importance of each quotation on their list. Students may use their books, notes, handouts, and most of all, group discussion. After two or three class periods, a spokesperson from each group presents the group's findings.

Here are the three lists I distribute to students:

List 1

Act I, scene 2: "Beware the Ides of March." [Soothsayer to Caesar]

Act I, scene 2: "No, Cassius, for the eye sees not itself but by reflection, by some other things." [Brutus to Cassius]

Act I, scene 2: "It doth amaze me a man of such a feeble temper should so get the start of the majestic world and bear the palm alone." [Cassius to Brutus]

Act I, scene 2: "Men at some time are masters of their fates." [Cassius to Brutus]

Act I, scene 2: "Yond Cassius has a lean and hungry look. He thinks too much; such men are dangerous." [Caesar to Antony]

List 2

Act I, scene 3: "But men may construe things after their fashion, clean from the purpose of the things themselves." [Cicero to Casca]

Act II, scene 1: "Which hatched would as his kind grow mischievous, and kill him in the shell." [Brutus to himself]

Act II, scene 1: "For Antony is but a limb of Caesar." [Brutus to the conspirators]

Act II, scene 1: "We all stand up against the spirit of Caesar." [Brutus to the conspirators]

Act II, scene 2: "Cowards die many times before their deaths; the valiant never taste of death but once." [Caesar to Calpurnia]

List 3

Act III, scene 1: "But I am as constant as the northern star." [Caesar to Cassius and Cinna]

Act III, scene 1: "I wish we may; but yet have I a mind that fears him much; and my misgivings still falls shrewdly to the purpose." [Cassius to Brutus]

Act III, scene 2: "I have the same dagger for myself when it shall please my country to need my death." [Brutus to the crowd]

Act IV, scene 3: "To tell thee that thou shalt see me at Philippi." [Caesar's spirit to Brutus]

Act V, scene 5: "I know my hour is come." [Brutus to Voluminous]

4. A wide choice of writing topics allows students to follow upon the aspect of *Julius Caesar* that each finds most intriguing. Here are writing topics I suggest after students have finished reading the play.

    Compose a letter to Brutus from Cassius advising him either to join or not to join the conspiracy.

    Write a journal as if from the perspective of one of the characters in the play, coordinating entries with significant events.

Write a definition of a hero or villain. Then choose someone
from the play who fulfills your definition; support your choice
in writing.

Choose a character whose actions were important in deter-
mining the outcome of the play. Think about how the chain
of events might have been affected if this character had acted
differently, and describe what different actions the character
might have taken and what the results might have been.

Through activities such as these, students come to realize that the study
of *Julius Caesar* is worth the challenge.

Sandra Bernstein, Oak Ridge High School, Conroe, Texas

The Red Badge of Courage

We never know how high we are
Till we are called to rise.

Emily Dickinson's words express that yearning, so strong in youth, to
test oneself. *The Red Badge of Courage* speaks to that yearning, just one
of the reasons for selecting this classic for study. But there are more. The
novel attracts students because it dramatizes breaking away from home.
It shows youth's resentment toward and need for authority. It tells how
one can be alone in the company of many. It reveals human weaknesses
like pride and cowardice as it shows our potential for heroism. It depicts
fear of failure and yet is a success story of sorts.

Teachers too have reasons for selecting *Red Badge*. The novel
provides an opportunity to examine closely certain elements of fiction,
especially style, multiple themes, character development, and the
relationship between mood and setting. Crane's work also serves as an
introduction to the psychological novel and has, in fact, been read by
many as a psychological study of fear. The book allows students to
discover truths about themselves and others and about life. Finally, the
book is short, and schedules sometimes preclude the consideration of
longer works.

Preliminary Small Group Activities

Divide the class into groups of four or five students and assign the following tasks. Each group later reports to the class on the results of its exploration, and the class responds with questions and comments.

1. Trace the events of the novel in sequence; note the time span of the novel as a whole.

2. Trace the steps in Henry's development from youth to man. How does his changing view of war reflect this maturation?

3. Record and categorize color images.

4. Identify figures of speech (metaphor, simile, personification) and group them into such categories as nature, machine, animal, religious, and so on.

5. Jot down typical examples of language used by the narrator, by Henry, and by other characters. What conclusions can be drawn?

6. Select several passages from the novel and list the verbs, adjectives, and nouns. Examine these lists. Do patterns emerge? What observations can you make?

Class Discussion

Although class editions of *Red Badge* usually contain helpful discussion questions and teachers have lists of their own, here are a few of the questions I regularly use. Insist that students cite evidence from the text to support their answers.

General Questions

1. What is the significance of the title? What does *red* symbolize? *badge?* How is Henry's red badge ironic? What is the meaning of *courage?* Are there different kinds of courage? Are courageous actions similar to/different from *brave, heroic, intrepid* ones? Are there circumstances under which a person might be more courageous than at other times? In a war or other disaster, are those who remain at home cowardly?

2. What is the effect of Crane's use of the general rather than the specific in character and place names and in time?

3. What statement about the relationship between man and nature does the novel make? You might consider images of fog, rain, and sun as a beginning.

4. In what ways are the novel and its protagonist affected by the fact that, excluding chapter one, no women are included? Would a writer today exclude women in a war novel?

Questions That Focus on the Protagonist

1. Why does Crane choose a fatherless youth as his protagonist?

2. What are the youth's feelings about the enemy? What are his feelings toward the officers? How do the officers feel/act toward their men?

3. Was Henry right in chapter one that "whatever he had learned of himself was here of no avail"? What does he discover about his physical self? moral self? social self? Is he disappointed or pleased with what he finds?

4. Itemize in specific terms what Henry learns from others and from each experience in battle.

5. At what times does Henry become "not a man but a member?" Can you recall times when you experienced this feeling? Did you think and act in the same way as you would have thought and acted as an individual?

6. Trace the parallels between the fighting and Henry's journey into "self." When does Henry talk banalities? When is he most pretentious? When does he seem to be rationalizing? Would Henry's maturing process have occurred so rapidly if he had remained at home?

7. Was Henry a hero or a coward?

Questions That Focus on the War

1. What factual information about this battle, this war, does the reader learn?

2. How does a civil war differ from a war against other nations?

3. Discuss Crane's image of war as "the blood-swollen god." Can you apply this idea to times other than war?

4. How does Crane differentiate between the popular view of war and the personal or private view?

Library Projects

These topics may be investigated by individuals or small groups. The results may be presented in writing, as panels and speeches, or as bulletin board displays.

1. Report on—or demonstrate—recent findings about how colors affect human beings. Can you apply these findings to Crane's use of color?

2. Build a case for *each* of the following: *The Red Badge of Courage* is an example of *naturalism, realism, romanticism, impressionism, all of the above, none of the above.*

3. Investigate the life of Stephen Crane and find out about some of his other works. "The Open Boat," "The Blue Hotel," and "The Bride Comes to Yellow Sky" are good possibilities if you're interested in short stories. You might also like to look at some of the poems in the collection *War Is Kind.*

4. Analyze Lincoln's Gettysburg address. Discuss its content, form, purpose, and style in relation to *Red Badge.*

5. Find out about impressionistic painting and music. Bring in examples to share with the class. Be prepared to lead a discussion of their relationship to each other and to Crane's style.

6. Read or reread William Golding's *Lord of the Flies.* What comparisons can you make with the corpse scene at the end of chapter seven of *Red Badge?* Are there other similarities between the two novels?

7. Read another Civil War novel. Compare it to *Red Badge* and draw conclusions. Possibilities include MacKinley Kantor's *Andersonville,* Margaret Mitchell's *Gone with the Wind,* Irene Hunt's *Across Five Aprils.*

8. Analyze war posters. Recruitment posters are an interesting possibility. Report to the class on your conclusions.

Writing Assignments

1. Recall a time you felt overpowering fear. Explain the circumstances. Analyze your reasons for fear. Describe the physical and emotional effects of that fear. What happened? Were your fears realized? Were you pleased with how you acted? Were you changed in any way by this experience?

2. Using *Red Badge* as a point of reference, consider the passage of time, how it can stand still or rush past. Include examples of this phenomenon from *Red Badge,* from other works you've read, and from personal experience. Draw a conclusion about the nature of time.

3. Describe Henry's mixed feelings in leaving home and mother. How does his mother feel? Why does she mention socks several times? Extend your observations to include similar experiences and reactions that apply to most young people and their parents.

4. Imagine that you are Henry. The battle has ended. Write a letter to your mother, a letter to a friend who stayed home, and a letter to the "dark girl."

5. Using Stephen Crane as your writing model, create a scene of your own for *Red Badge.*

6. Write a news report of the battle. Then write an editorial and a human interest story. You may add details of your own invention.

7. Adapt *one* of the preliminary small group activities, class discussion questions, or library research projects as the subject for an essay. After you have done some preliminary thinking, discuss your choice with your teacher.

Follow-up Small Group Activities

1. Prepare a reading of one or more passages from the novel. Be attentive to the sounds and rhythms of language and how these elements enhance images called forth by the words.

2. Dramatize (or pantomime) a scene from the novel. Use props and/or background music if you wish.

3. Compose and perform for the class a folk song or a dance that relates to the events of or a scene from the novel.

4. Represent the novel through a watercolor, drawing, collage, or poster.

5. Relate the novel to contemporary times through an editorial cartoon or a comic strip.

6. You are the director in charge of filming the novel. How will you cast it? How will you handle the camera? What do you have in

mind for setting and sound? Will you make symbolic use of color? How?

7.   Assemble a slide/tape presentation that depicts a theme from the novel. You might consider presenting that theme in contemporary terms.

8.   Interview several people from different age groups who have served in wars. Think carefully about the questions you will ask. Support your findings and conclusions in writing or as a panel discussion.

Beverly Haley, The Language Works, Fort Morgan, Colorado

The Grapes of Wrath

In January of 1939 John Steinbeck was exhausted—and fearful. Worn by what he called "thousands of hours" of research and writing, he spent two weeks in bed worrying about his latest completed manuscript.

Steinbeck was both wrong and right to worry. *The Grapes of Wrath* swept the best-seller lists of those last years of the Great Depression partly because of its appeal as a historical novel. But its popularity was and is tied to controversy; for nearly fifty years it has been attacked for its use of language, for its realism, and for its politics.

English teachers know the hazards of teaching *The Grapes of Wrath*—the controversies, the length, the reading ability and maturity of their students. They also know that Steinbeck won a Nobel Prize and that his novel won a Pulitzer Prize; they know that the book is included in the list of classics that the National Endowment for the Humanities believes high school students should read. And they know that careful reading and discussion, especially in a classroom of mature juniors and seniors, are important in understanding controversial classics.

Plan to spend at least seventeen days with this many-faceted novel.

Suggested Schedule

Days 1–3	Introduction to the novel, including a discussion of Steinbeck and the Okies, the geography of the book, and time for reading
Day 4	Explaining and assigning the position paper

Days 5–7	Reading and reviewing events of the Great Depression
Days 8–10	Discussing the Steinbeck style and "phalanx theory" through supplementary reading; reading the novel
Day 11	Discussing Steinbeck and the Nobel and Pulitzer prizes
Days 12–14	Prewriting, drafting, anecdotal research; reading the novel
Days 15–16	Films: *The Great American Novel: The Grapes of Wrath* (Columbia Broadcasting System, 1967) and *The Grapes of Wrath* (Fox, 1940)
Day 17	Paper due with time for in-class proofreading

The first three days should provide background for the novel as well as time for reading. Remind students that Steinbeck began his research on migrants in 1936, when he wrote a series of articles for the San Francisco *News,* an exposé of California workers who came primarily from Oklahoma and Arkansas. Then in 1937 he toured the Oklahoma Dust Bowl and in 1938 visited migrant camps in California.

Refer to the dedication: Carol is Steinbeck's wife, who both typed the novel and suggested its title—a Civil War song. Remind students that this was a highly controversial book that offended both Californians and Oklahomans, who thought it was a slanted, ugly picture of their states. Then define the basic plot—the Joad family move from the Dust Bowl of Oklahoma—using a map of the United States. (There are maps of both Steinbeck's California and the Joads' trek in my *Writing Seminars in the Content Area: In Search of Hemingway, Salinger, and Steinbeck,* a publication available from NCTE.) Finally, point to Steinbeck's use of interchapters that divide the plot and convey his anger, philosophy, and compassion for the Okies. Perhaps one interchapter should be read aloud.

The assignment on Day 4 is crucial to the success of the entire project. Students are asked to begin work on a three- to five-page position paper in which they limit their analysis of the novel to a single focus. This position is to be organized, supported by concrete detail, and mechanically sound. Here are some of the position suggestions I offer, which students are free to accept, reject, or adapt.

1.   What is the meaning of "family" in this book?

2. One critic said: The book is a "story of the awakening of a man's conscience." Is it? Whose conscience?

3. Is this book an attack on America? Is Steinbeck advocating socialism? Is the government camp a symbol?

4. What is the meaning of the land? Remember that the land, the American "good earth," was so important to Americans in 1939— and now.

5. Discuss the ending—so vivid and controversial.

6. Answer those critics who want to ban this book from high schools.

By Day 5 students should have read a good chunk of the novel. Now is the time to place the artifact in its historical setting. Using the chalkboard, develop a 1930s chronology: begin with the 1929 stock market crash, move through FDR's New Deal pledge in 1932 and his 100 days of 1933, from the 1935 Dust Bowl and the 1937 migration to the beginning of World War II in 1939. Days 6 and 7 can give reinforcement with films, like *Life in the Thirties* (NBC, 1959); filmstrips, like *Grapes of Wrath and the 1930s*; records, like Woody Guthrie's *Dust Bowl Blues*; or books, like Studs Terkel's *Hard Times* (Washington Square Press, 1978) oral histories. (Also: with student assistance, develop a bulletin board and a class library with 1930s artifacts and good photographic materials, such as the Time-Life *Fabulous Century* volumes.) Here maybe the time to use community people who remember the 1930s.

Days 8 to 10 are a crucial time. Students are deep into the novel. Now is a time to reflect on Steinbeck's style and mind and to return to the idea of a position paper. Instead of reading from *The Grapes of Wrath*, I select one of the following stories to read aloud: "The Harness," "The Snake," or "Breakfast." Through discussion we piece together the Steinbeck who was sensitive to nature, who believed himself to be "a scientist of the imagination." Ask students: "If you had to write a paper on this story, what would be your position?" We go on to consider how we might document and organize that position based on the story we just read. On day 10, I add theory, Steinbeck's (and that of his friend Ed Ricketts—The Doc in "The Snake") concept of the "phalanx": groups are separate and distinct from the individuals that compose them, yet the groups have transcendent power because people often behave on the basis of the group nature. Thus the Joads' movement westward is a phalanx, as in the movement of the Okies. The Californians, who as a group oppose the

Okies but may relent as individuals, form a phalanx. Some observers note that the turtle of the novel is also a tortoise or *testudo*, the same word for the ancient Roman *phalanx*—a close order of advancing soldiers with shields locked overhead.

Day 11 honors Steinbeck's receipt of the Pulitzer Prize in 1940, which was instrumental in his winning of the 1962 Nobel Prize. You may wish to refer to W. J. Stuckey's *The Pulitzer Prize Novels* (University of Oklahoma Press) and to *American Winners of the Nobel Literary Prize*, edited by Warren G. French and Walter E. Kidd (University Microfilms International). This is a good time to discuss awards and prizes that both delight and frighten authors. While the Swedish Academy called Steinbeck a "bold observer of human behavior," the author was always shy and fearful of prizes—especially the Nobel, which he felt was the kiss of death.

By Day 12 the students should be nearly finished reading the novel. Now we spend time talking about how we write, how we get ideas. Students also share the positions that they are developing in their papers.

Days 13 and 14 deal with an important decision: who is this man, John Steinbeck? I ask students to do some simple research about the man behind the book. For this purpose I assemble in the classroom as much Steinbeck material as I can from public, school, and personal libraries, from friends and colleagues and students, from old textbooks—his collected letters, biographies, newspaper and magazine clippings, the recording of him reading "Johnny Bear," posters and pictures. Each student finds an anecdote to share with the class. On Day 14 students tell stories about Steinbeck's life long interest in King Arthur, his love of dogs, his college pranks, his wonderful letters, his red pony, his relationship with his wives and sons.

The book is read. The prewriting, drafting, and documenting are nearly over. Perhaps now is the time for a final visual statement. On Days 15 and 16 I have used John Ford's 1940 *Grapes of Wrath* (now available in videotape), which Steinbeck called "hard, truthful." Or the educational film *The Great American Novel: The Grapes of Wrath* can offer twenty-five minutes of thoughtful parallels between 1930s Okies and modern migrants.

On Day 17, with time for in-class proofreading, the position papers are collected. (Some instructors may prefer to collect them before the film, then grade and return them on Day 17.) While the position paper could end the unit, let me suggest an alternative: Select three or four papers to be shared with the class the following day. Have the writers read their papers aloud, and let the class determine the position of each paper and comment on the clarity and support of each.

After these seventeen days, *The Grapes of Wrath* is no longer just a title. It is, as one of my students said, "an achievement." Through a logical progression, this classic has been discovered: its complex plot and its tie to history, its author and his lyrical passion to arouse humankind, its enduring popularity and its controversial nature. Through reading and writing and discussion, the book has come alive. Perhaps some readers' nerves have been tested, and perhaps some are still not satisfied. But all that may be the final achievement of a classic.

Brooke Workman, West High School, Iowa City, Iowa

Macbeth

Fair is foul, and foul is fair.

So said the trio of witches. What better way to introduce the Shakespeare tragedy of *Macbeth* than with a discussion of how this quotation fits the 1980s socially, politically, and morally? The violence and ruthlessness of *Macbeth* match anything students see in the evening news or at the movies. The current appeal of the occult ties neatly into Shakespeare's use of ghosts, witches, and apparitions. The question of what is "manly" and what is "womanly" is hotly discussed daily, and the issues of suicide and of madness are as relevant today as they were in Shakespeare's time.

The thematic elements in *Macbeth*—motivations of fear, guilt, pride, revenge; the dangers incurred in going against human and natural laws; the perversion of ambition to insatiable greed—all these have modern application, both social and personal.

While we want our students to read, understand, and enjoy at least one Shakespeare play in their high school years, students often resist the unfamiliar language and the discipline required to read such a work. Some college instructors advise us to leave Shakespeare to them. But high school students deserve the chance to appreciate Shakespeare's drama and language.

The following questions and activities are suggested to complement your presentation of the play. Used in conjunction with reading and analysis, they offer your students the chance to explore the play more fully, in tasks that range from drawing an editorial cartoon of one of the scenes to keeping a notebook of favorite passages.

Discussion Questions

Here are a few questions that I regularly use in discussing *Macbeth*. I insist that students cite evidence from the text to support their answers.

1. Is Macbeth the "hero" or the "villain" in this tragedy? How do the kings Duncan and Malcolm compare in strength and in nobility to Macbeth?

2. What effect does not knowing Lady Macbeth's first name have on the reader? What is the significance of the manner in which Lady Macbeth commits suicide? Do her madness and her act of suicide indicate that she no longer is the strong character she appeared to be the earlier portions of the play? Why or why not?

3. What is Shakespeare's purpose in devoting so much of the play to the ideal of "manliness"? According to the dialogue, the events, and the themes of the play, what are the qualities of being a "man"? Is "manliness" synonymous with "bravery"? Explore this idea by finding specific passages in the play that relate to the idea of manliness and interpret these passages within the context of the play.

4. Are the witches real or imagined? How do you know? Who or what are they? Why are the witches sometimes referred to as the "weird sisters"? Who uses this term? What is the significance of the fact that the witches are seen first in a deserted place and later in a cavern? Where do the witches draw the line about how much they will tell Macbeth? Why? What does Macbeth's response reveal about the change in his attitude toward them (as compared with the first witch scene) and toward himself as well?

5. What is Macbeth's outlook on life? Cite a passage and explain.

Small Group Activities

Divide the class into small groups, and let each group pick one of the following tasks. Provide space for displaying art projects and class time for group presentations.

1. Use your artistic talents to sketch sets or costumes; make posters advertising a production of the play; prepare a collage, a diorama of a scene, or papier-mâché masks for several characters; or draw an editorial cartoon or a comic strip.

2. Prepare an interpretation of one of the scenes using dance or mime. Provide background music, costumes, and lighting for your performance.

3. Research the political and historical state of Scotland at the time the play is set; the history of witchcraft and its status today; "offbeat" or unusual productions of *Macbeth*, and popular and critical responses to these productions; the history and location of well-known castles in Scotland.

4. Devise a readers-theatre production of a scene or series of scenes; a costumed dramatization of a scene of your choice; a debate on a topic such as "Ambition is a positive quality of a leader" or "Lady Macbeth is more 'manly' than her husband."

5. Select an activity related to *Macbeth* that you feel matches the others in creativity and amount of work.

Activities for Individuals or Pairs of Students

Students can work on these activities either individually or paired with another student. Encourage students to find an interesting way to present their findings and conclusions to the rest of the class.

1. Look through the stage directions and the dialogue for details about setting, particularly those that show the isolation of the place, light and darkness, sounds and silences, cold, and physical descriptions. Then draw conclusions about how the setting complements, contrasts, or reveals the play's action, characters, and themes.

2. Make a log of particular examples of metaphors. Put the metaphors into categories, such as *clothing, health, color, life, death,* and *time.* How do the metaphors enhance the play's themes?

3. Find examples of Shakespeare's use of irony, paradox, and puns. Do you see any common themes? What is the total effect?

4. Record any allusions to mythological characters and to passages from the Bible. Explain how each is used in the context of the play.

5. Prepare a notebook of your favorite passages from *Macbeth*. At the end of each entry, write a brief statement telling why you chose this passage.

Ideas for Writing Assignments

1. Write an essay on the power of one man's greed affecting an entire people's welfare.

2. Trace the ways in which loyalty to the king is seen as a value throughout *Macbeth*. Or write an essay that illustrates your personal views about loyalty to the government, to family, to friends, or to an ideal, with references to the loyalty themes found in *Macbeth*.

3. Trace the change in the other characters' views of Macbeth, citing particular passages in their chronological order and commenting on the possible reasons behind those changes.

4. Compare and contrast the major changes in the two main characters, Macbeth and Lady Macbeth, as the play progresses.

Creative Writing

1. After reading Macbeth's "Life is but a shadow" passage, write your own version of the theme as it relates to your personal views.

2. Assume the role of Lady Macbeth's doctor. Write your report and interpretation of her sleepwalking episode. Now write a modern doctor's version of the same report.

3. Create one or more "underground" fliers designed to stir up a revolution against Macbeth.

4. Think of several expressions that convey the same idea as the one referred to in the play: "The cat would eat fish, but she will not wet her feet." Or write riddles similar to those the witches posed to Macbeth.

Beverly Haley, Fort Morgan, Colorado

Using *Fahrenheit 451* to Debate Censorship

Several years ago I heard Ray Bradbury tell a spellbound audience of high school students how he wrote his first novel, *Fahrenheit 451*, on a coin-operated typewriter in a library basement. Afterwards, I reread several of his works and decided to teach *Fahrenheit 451*, concentrating on the theme of censorship, to a class of junior students with low to average ability.

While students were reading the first of the novel's three sections, I focused classroom discussion on language usage and the structure of the novel, including plot, characterization, and setting. The low reading level and simple plot structure in contrast with extensive use of figurative language techniques in the narrative make *Fahrenheit 451* an ideal vehicle to teach or review metaphor, simile, and allusion.

When students were ready to move on to Parts Two and Three, I shifted our focus to Bradbury's theme of censorship versus the freedom to read. Our analysis began with list making. Students used their books to find all the different types of media which Bradbury mentions being censored. (More recently, students called my attention to a type Bradbury missed: music video censorship.) Students agreed that in *Fahrenheit 451* most of our common forms of communication are illegal except under strict supervision and in digest form.

Next, students reviewed the text for Bradbury's opinion of censorship. They found helpful the conversation between Montag and Beatty in which Beatty tells the history of censorship (pp. 57–67 in the 1979 Ballantine edition) as well as Faber's analysis of conditions leading to his lost job as English teacher (pp. 96–97). As students stated Beatty's reasons for censorship, I listed them on the chalkboard:

> cut long books to summaries because people had no time to read books
>
> cut courses like English and history out of curriculum
>
> close theaters
>
> use more pictures and cartoons
>
> omit anything objectionable to minorities
>
> censor any controversial or thought-provoking ideas

To this list students added other reasons for censorship. They mentioned that Bradbury's world does not censor pornography and ours does. I defined the phrase *without redeeming social value* and the words *slander* and *libel* before adding them to our list.

Through anecdote and questioning, I called students' attention to the differences between total and partial censorship. I pointed out that parts of a book may be taken out as unsuitable, or a book or magazine may be called unsuitable for readers under a certain age. Other books are censored by being unobtainable in certain parts of the country. I explained that because of unflattering descriptions, *Grapes of Wrath* was not in the local library collection when I was growing up in Oklahoma. More recently Waukegan, Illinois, schools took *Huck Finn* off the shelves after local protests. As part of our discussion, we considered Bradbury's comment that no writer can please every segment of an audience.

The class concluded their investigation of censorship by examining Bradbury's own words. Our edition of *Fahrenheit 451* contains an afterword in which Bradbury tells of censorship of his own work. Ironically, editors of this edition cut seventy-five bits and pieces from editions of *Fahrenheit 451* in the years since its first publication in 1953. Students were amazed to discover that the innocent language of the novel that they read had been subjected to censorship in earlier versions. Reading the afterword gave students the author's view of the sanctity of his writing. As Bradbury concludes, "I will not go gently onto a shelf, degutted, to become a non-book" (p.184).

By this time the class was ready to attack the problem of censorship from a different perspective. I assigned the students the problem of responding to censorship of a novel. Students were allowed to choose *Fahrenheit 451* or a novel read earlier in the semester. The assignment was to write a letter to the novel's author or publisher or to a newspaper in reply to supposed censorship. Students could argue for or against censoring all or parts of a book or could explain why the book in question should not be censored. I gave each student a copy of the instructions below, a list of novels to choose from, and a summary of topics in those novels that might be likely to come under fire. I also supplied students with a review of censorship problems in *Huck Finn* as a sample of the type of writing they were to produce. A useful resource at this point was *Celebrating Censored Books* (Wisconsin Council of Teachers of English, 1985), which gives examples of replies to censorship.

Censorship Writing Assignment

1. Working with a partner, choose one of these books that you both have read. You will each need to find a copy of the chosen book to use as a reference.

The Contender	*To Kill a Mockingbird*
The Outsiders	*Of Mice and Men*
A Separate Peace	*Durango Street*
Lord of the Flies	*Fahrenheit 451*
West Side Story	

2. Working together, make a list of all the reasons your book could be censored. Next to each reason describe or quote the exact part of the book which is censorable for that reason. These reasons for censorship could include language, racism, prejudice of some other sort, violence, criticism of government, criticism of religion, sex, use of drugs, suicide, and antipatriotic or antiwar messages.

3. Write a letter to the book's author or publisher or to a newspaper explaining why this book should or should not be censored. You may choose to defend the book or to censor it. Your position does not necessarily have to be one you agree with. In writing your letter, use the reasons from your list.

    If you are writing in support of censorship, explain what ideas or elements are offensive and tell why. Use specific examples from the book. Also explain why it would be harmful for others to read the book.

If you are writing in an effort to abolish (get rid of) censorship, explain what issues others have found offensive and give their reasons. Then explain why you feel the book should not be censored. Give reasons why other people should read the book.

Your letter should be about two pages in length. It should be well written, properly addressed, and neatly completed. You must turn in all your work, including your list, notes, first draft, and final copy.

I assigned the writing of a first draft for homework. In class the next day, pairs of students met again and exchanged papers to read and edit. Students spent two days on prewriting and fifteen to thirty minutes on editing.

Writing about a specific example of censorship fulfills several objectives. Bradbury's novel acquires relevance as students see censorship as an element in their lives. This open-ended assignment allows students latitude in the use of style and tone. Better writers use satire effectively in protesting against a novel; and less able writers feel secure in using a familiar novel in order to discuss censorship. Students practice the real-life skills of examining an issue and organizing a paper presenting the evidence from a specific viewpoint.

I have repeated this exercise several times, and each time I am pleasantly surprised at how well students succeed with their papers.

Jill Martin, Warren Township High School, Lake Forest, Illinois

A Tale of Two Cities: Dickens and Historical Perspective

The place of Dickens in high school British Literature courses seems secure. The question is not so much *whether* to read Dickens, as it is *which* of his works to read? Many opt for *Great Expectations,* perhaps because it is the most tightly written of his novels. An older favorite, though less structured and lapsing sometimes into Victorian sentimentality, may deserve another look. *A Tale of Two Cities,* with its historical panorama and detailed verbal picturization, can be a very effective tool for drawing a class not only into Dickens's art but also into the political conflicts of his era.

"It was the best of times; it was the worst of times." The profound ambiguity that Dickens felt towards both the historical events and his characters in this novel is apparent from its opening words. The evils of the *ancien régime* are detailed in such episodes as the death of the little girl under the speeding wheels of the Marquis's coach. The excesses of the Republic are as apparent not only in the butchery of the prisoners but also in the guillotining of the little seamstress who is as much an innocent victim as the girl.

Their criminal insensitivity to the plight of the impoverished cannot deprive the imprisoned aristocrats of dignity as they face their impending doom with restraint and evening entertainments. Nor can the justice of her cause excuse Madame Defarge's insistence that not only Charles Darnay but also Lucie and her daughter must die as well. Both social classes share the same flow in Dickens's eyes. "The two regimes of France—the old order of the Marquis St. Evremonde and the new of the revolutionary Defarges—exalt their class, their abstract principles, above . . . personal ethics" (Angus Wilson, *The World of Charles Dickens,* New York: The Viking Press, 1970, p. 262). Perhaps by studying briefly those abstract principles, students can see and appreciate more clearly the fatal blindness that afflicts almost all of Dickens's characters in this novel.

First Phase: Background

To prepare the students for reading the novel intelligently, a great deal of background is necessary. Students with different interests and abilities can volunteer for or be assigned to appropriate prereading projects designed to provide a schema for understanding the novel. They can readily investigate certain key historical elements and prepare posters and handouts for in-class presentations. A time line charting the key events of 1770 to 1790 is helpful, as is a chart of the titles and hierarchy of the British and French nobilities and of the structure of each government. A graph showing the distribution of wealth within the population, perhaps contrasted with a similar one for contemporary America, would reveal the differences between the diverse societies. A model guillotine helps too, as would a model of the Bastille.

As the final stage of preparation, the students should receive the *Declaration on the Rights of Man and of the Citizen* adopted by the French National Assembly on August 29, 1789 (available from the Encyclopedia Britannica). Subsequent class discussion can focus on the contrast between this declaration and the American Declaration of Independence. Especially effective is paralleling on the chalkboard the rights detailed by the American Bill of Rights and the French Declaration.

Second Phase: Reading the Novel

Because of the length of the work, three visual techniques can help keep student interest up.

First, a map of the territory between London and Paris can be prepared as a useful graphic organizer. Moving markers of different shapes or colors can provide a sense of location for each character as the action shifts from place to place.

Second, organizing a list of "doubles" on the board (cities, trials, mobs, and so on) and adding to it section by section as the book is read can sensitize students to Dickens's underlying structure.

Third, organizing lists of parallel images in the same way can sensitize students to that element in Dickens's art. The color red, sounds, roads— these are three easily recognized and very important recurring images.

Third Phase: Reactions

The first strategy for generating student writing about the novel would be to use the lists of doubles and images to explore concrete themes in an organized way. This approach would give students an excellent chance to practice simple writing. Or, a more imaginative approach would be student narratives in which students placed themselves at the foot of the guillotine, for example.

A second strategy would be to compare and contrast this novel with others dealing with the same or similar historical events and attitudes. *The Scarlet Pimpernel* comes immediately to mind, though some revolutionary novels of the twentieth century might also be appropriate. Possibilities might include Chinua Achebe's *Things Fall Apart,* Maya Angelou's *I Know Why the Caged Bird Sings,* Ernest Hemingway's *For Whom the Bell Tolls,* John Steinbeck's *The Grapes of Wrath,* and Richard Wright's *Native Son.* Videocassettes of film adaptations of some of these novels are available.

Students can delve further into historical evaluation or critical thinking through a third technique for generating student reaction, based on Dickens's depiction of women in the novel. Dickens is ambiguous about the events and the characters in this novel because he knew from his reading of history that both French regimes had been blind to their own failings. From the perspective of contemporary issues, the same charge could be levied against Dickens himself. His women characters are dominated by men. The only exception is Madame Defarge, whose liberation has created a monster.

The students may receive a copy of the Seneca Falls Declaration of Sentiments and Resolutions on Woman's Rights of July 19, 1848. (Available in H. S. Commager's *Documents of American History* (Appleton, Century, Crofts, 1973). When contrasted with the previous documents, this declaration reveals one point very clearly. The rights being claimed are no longer merely political and economic but profoundly personal: education, moral independence, and self-fulfillment. From a contemporary viewpoint, the document is an amazing foreshadowing of much of the feminist movement. (An important historical footnote is that one third of the signers of this declaration were men.)

Students could explore Dickens's presuppositions about the role of women in society. Which women does he seem to admire? Which women appeal to us today? Have standards for men changed in a similar way?

Interested students could also research the British or American suffragettes and contrast these women with those in this novel. Which kind of woman came to dominate the later struggle for women's rights?

The same lesson of the moral ambiguity of all revolutions could be pursued into other areas of literature. Works dealing with racism, sexual liberation, and so on are widely available. Without proselytizing, we can help our students become more aware of the great conflicts that face our century, just as Dickens dealt with those of his age.

> *A Tale of Two Cities* is a profoundly thoughtful, if not a theoretical book. It is the sort of novel that should be enormously usable for young people and their teachers. . . . Its conception can vivify for us the meanings of the past, can offer us a reading of history, humane and deep, by a great artistic intelligence. (G. Robert Strange, "Dickens and the Fiery Past," *20th Century Interpretations of* A Tale of Two Cities, Prentice-Hall, Inc., 1972, p. 75.)

Michael Marchal, Saint Xavier High School, Cincinnati, Ohio, and John Hussong, Saint Xavier High School, Cincinnati, Ohio

Literature Assignment of the Month

The Nature of Love: Two Short Stories

> *... Young men's love then lies*
> *Not truly in their hearts, but in their eyes.*
> —William Shakespeare, *Romeo and Juliet*

Probably no topic fascinates teenagers quite as much as the relationships between the sexes—not sports or automobiles or rock groups. Yet their information about pop stars, athletes, and cars far exceeds their understanding of love. It's not surprising, therefore, that young adults are drawn to literature that explores the concept of love. John Collier's "The Chaser" and Max Shulman's "Love Is a Fallacy" both speak to the romantic notions of youth concerning love and marriage. Both stories document the effects of attempting to change another person to conform to one's own notion of an ideal relationship. In Collier's story, students see the devastating results of a one-sided relationship based on absolute devotion. In Shulman's story, they see how love can sometimes defy logical analysis. Both stories make clear that true love involves more than our own limited and often selfish desires and interests.

But there are other reasons for selecting these stories. They allow students to discover truths about their own views of love and to gain insight into the views of others. These two stories can also serve as an introduction to more complex works of literature that deal with the nature of love. Finally, both stories provide an opportunity to examine closely a key element of fiction—irony.

The Opinionnaire: How Students View Love

I begin with an activity that relies on a simple idea: students have opinions about love. Before I assign the stories, therefore, I ask students to react to the statements reproduced below.

True Love Opinionnaire

Directions: Read each of the following statements. Write *A* if you agree with a statement or *D* if you disagree with a statement.

1. If you really care for someone, there is nothing wrong with doing whatever you have to do, even lying, to get that person to love you.

2. If you are really in love, the longer you and your partner are together, the stronger your love grows.

3. True lovers should never flirt with other people of the opposite sex.

4. It is never right to scheme just to get someone you like to go out with you.

5. True lovers should spend as much time together as possible.

6. If you are really in love, physical appearance does not matter.

7. It is never right to go out with someone just because he or she is popular or attractive.

8. Physical attraction must come before true love.

9. True lovers should have different opinions and interests.

10. True love means sometimes doing things your partner wants to do even when you don't want to, like going on a picnic when you'd rather see a good movie.

After the class has completed the opinionnaire, I lead a discussion that focuses on their responses to each statement. I encourage students to clarify their answers and to debate their differences. I also provide synthesis and direction. Because the statements require students to take a stand, a lively discussion ensues.

The purpose of the opinionnaire and the follow-up discussion, of course, is to create interest in the characters and issues in the stories students are about to read. Items 5 and 9, for example, relate to one aspect of the problem faced by Alan, the main character in "The Chaser." Alan finds the effects of the love potion appealing because the woman he desires will then want nothing but solitude and him. Responses to these items suggest that many students also think such a relationship is what they want. The old man in Collier's story, however, suggests that this situation will become intolerable. Through class discussion of the opinionnaire, students begin to question some of their initial responses and are consequently prepared to analyze this theme in the stories they are about to read.

After students have read both stories, I divide the class into small, mixed groups and ask them to determine from evidence in the stories how Alan and Petey would define love. How does the narrator of "Fallacy" view love? I ask each group to present to the class its definitions along with supporting evidence from the stories. To help the groups get started, I ask how Polly would define love. Most students quickly see that her view is based on appearances. As evidence, they point to the last line of the story: "He's got a raccoon coat." Later, the class reassembles to discuss its findings.

What Irony Reveals

After students understand what love means to the characters in the two stories, they are prepared to deal with irony—the implicit view of love behind the explicit one. What are the authors really telling us about love?

I ask students to return to their small groups and to attempt to explain why the views of love held by Alan and the narrator of "Fallacy" will prove inadequate. What are Collier and Shulman trying to tell us about the nature of love? In working out answers to these questions, students begin to understand that it is irony that provides the link between each character's limited view of love and the more mature view offered by the authors.

Again, the class reassembles to discuss and debate its findings. Gradually, students begin to formulate important conclusions. They realize, for example, that Collier is criticizing more than Alan's romanticized notion that Diane should be jealous of other women. They perceive that Collier is really telling us that love involves considering the needs of people to be free. They recognize that if Alan's ideal were realized, it would result in an unbearable chaining of one individual to another.

Following this discussion, I ask students to refer back to the opinionnaire and to compare their responses with their observations about the stories. Often opinions have changed. It is not surprising to hear a student say, "I guess it isn't always a good idea to spend all of your time with the person you love."

Follow-up Evaluation

To learn how well students have understood the ironic technique, I ask them to read on their own another story that involves the concept of love and that relies on irony to convey its meaning. Then I ask them to write an interpretation of that story. A good story to use is O. Henry's "The Exact Science of Matrimony." This follow-up reinforces skills students have developed in reading and analyzing "The Chaser" and "Love Is a Fallacy"; it also serves as an evaluation of their mastery of those skills.

Larry R. Johannessen, Lyons Township High School, La Grange, Illinois

Sensitizing Students to Technique

It's often difficult for students to discern and understand the techniques that authors use to motivate readers. The following lesson uses reading and writing activities to accomplish this goal for George Orwell's classic essay "Marrakech." The benefits to the success of this approach are threefold. First, it prepares and motivates students to want to read the essay on their own. Second, it provides support during their reading. Finally, it gives students the opportunity to synthesize what they have learned and to extend and apply this knowledge.

I begin by suggesting to students that on any given day, all of us may wish that we were someplace other than a classroom. I then ask students to close their eyes and to visualize a place they would like to be at that moment. I ask questions similar to the following ones to help guide the creation of their images: "Where are you? What people do you see? What colors dominate this scene? What are you doing in this scene? What are you saying?"

After students have had their eyes closed for a minute or two, I ask them to open their eyes and to write nonstop for five minutes, describing the scene they have been imagining. Then students look at what they have written and attempt to collapse it into one sentence that capsulizes the essence of their image. To find out how effective their sentences are, students form pairs and read their sentences aloud. The student listener describes the images that come to mind, and then the two students discuss the discrepancies between the image intended by the writer and the image perceived by the listener. The partners then switch roles and repeat the process.

After volunteers read their writings to the class, we talk about the exercise and about the difficulty of capturing the essence of a place in just one sentence. Then we move on to the next step in the lesson.

I ask students if any of them have ever seen such movies as *Casablanca*, *Raiders of the Lost Ark*, *Romancing the Stone*, or *Murder on the Orient Express*, and what it is that attracts most of us to these movies. Students usually identify factors such as the following, which I list on the chalkboard:

> Movies like these portray adventure and suspense that most of us don't have in our lives.

> Many of these movies portray an elegant way of life that we might like but that is beyond our means.

> We are attracted to the romance of visiting exotic, faraway places.

I then explain to students what I believe to be one of the ironies of watching such movies: these movies leave us with positive feelings despite the fact that alongside the images of adventure and excitement, most show a great number of negative images of life as well, images of poverty, violence, oppression, disease, and death. With this in mind, students examine the opening paragraph of Orwell's essay, "Marrakech," written about a supposed exotic place not far from Casablanca. I use a transparency to show students this one-sentence paragraph. Doing so helps to heighten the effect this paragraph has on students.

> As the corpse went past, the flies left the restaurant table in a cloud and rushed after it, but they came back a few minutes later.

Students are usually stunned by the harshness of this image. I ask them what Orwell reveals in this one sentence about the quality of human life in Marrakech. Initial responses are typically vague, but students agree that this image suggests that the quality of life is not high. As we continue to examine this passage, students discover that there is a lot that is implied in the text. A dead corpse should be a feast for flies, but since the flies come back to the table, students surmise, the corpse must not have provided the flies with much nourishment. Thus, if even a dead body has nothing much to offer flies, what can life be like for the living? I record this and other observations on the chalkboard.

When I ask students what provides the fuel for their observations, they readily recognize that it is Orwell's careful selection of detail that leads them to the observations they make. When I ask if it is easy to select just the right details to create a desired impression, students consider the difficulty they had in writing a one-sentence description, and agree that it isn't as easy as they had thought.

I then point out that this is one of the artistic merits of Orwell's essay. He carefully selects details so that instead of just telling us what he saw, he helps us see it ourselves and draw the desired conclusions.

Finally, I specify a purpose for students' reading of Orwell's essay. I ask students to examine not only what Orwell says about the situation in Marrakech—that what people think they see is in sharp contrast with the harsh reality—but also how he says it, i.e., how he makes the reader see and feel what he sees and feels.

I ask students to write a brief "reader response" to their initial reading of the essay. (This response is guided by questions based on the work of David Bleich.) I also provide a study guide that helps guide students' exploration. I prefer to ask students to complete the study guide during a second reading because I want them to learn that to really understand something you read, you have to read it more than once. However, there is no reason why students couldn't complete the study guide as they read the essay and then write a reader response after they have finished the study guide. This way they can use the reader response as a way to summarize their reactions to what they have just read.

Reader Response

First, read George Orwell's "Marrakech" for enjoyment. Immediately after you finish reading, answer the following questions "off the top of your head." Spend between five and ten minutes on your responses.

1. Respond emotionally. How do you feel about what you've read? Bored? Excited? Depressed? Ready to go out and change the world? Confused? In a paragraph or so, describe your emotional response in detail.

2. Make associations with what you've read, based on your own experience. Push until you have thought of at least five associations involving similar experiences or previous times when you felt this way.

3. Find a word (or words), a passage, or a feature of the selection that caught your attention. If you like a phrase or a sentence, write it down. Try to determine why you like it. If you're confused about

something, isolate it and make a note of the page number or line. Phrase a question to ask a classmate, to ask in class, or to ask me.

Study Guide

After you've finished your reader response, reexamine the essay. For each of the designated sections of the essay, answer the questions as best you can.

The introduction

1. What statement is Orwell trying to make?
2. How is he making his statement?

The scene with the gazelles

1. What statement is Orwell trying to make?
2. How is he making his statement?

The scene in the ghetto

1. What statement is Orwell trying to make?
2. How is he making his statement?

The scene with the elderly woman

1. What statement is Orwell trying to make?
2. How is he making his statement?

The scene with the black soldiers

1. What statement is Orwell trying to make?
2. How is he making his statement?

Students have told me that they might have avoided reading "Marrakech" if I had just asked them to "read it for tomorrow." Because of what we did in class, however, students say they felt compelled to read the essay. Also, when students have completed the reader response and the study guide, they are prepared to come to class and discuss the essay with authority. I always find the discussion following the reading to be lively and insightful, and I often learn something new about the essay from students. After this discussion, students find it easier to write a paper on Orwell's essay. The information and insight they have gained give them confidence that they have something to say, especially about the techniques that Orwell uses to affect the reaction of his readers.

Edgar Thompson, Christiansburg, Virginia

Proverbs as Literature

Often we take for granted the idea that literature is transcribed language, and neglect oral tradition by concentrating solely on written forms. This is a particularly unfortunate oversight when it comes to exploring African culture since so much of it is embodied in oral tradition.

African folktales and oral tradition are available to American students in various forms, from children's books to epic poetry. For high school, some of these forms may be either too juvenile or discouragingly lengthy. Why not turn, as I did, to the African proverb? The proverb offers an intriguing glimpse into the "worldview" of African cultures. The crisp, often jarring, images are a stimulating preparation for further encounters with African literature. Used as much today as in the past, proverbs give a sense of transition from the traditional to the modern—a theme very common in African poetry, fiction, and drama.

Despite their succinctness and imagery, proverbs can be difficult to understand on more than one level. I present proverbs to my students as challenging brainteasers, with the help of a technique developed at the Institute of Cultural Affairs in Chicago, Illinois. In "guided conversations," students move through four levels of meaning, from the obvious to the symbolic. The four levels are referred to as the *Objective, Reflective, Interpretive,* and *Decisional.* In a typical lesson using this technique, I read a proverb aloud several times and then pose questions to prompt discussion at the four levels. For example, I often use the Senegalese proverb and the discussion questions shown below.

> *Eat to please yourself but dress to please others.*

Objective Question
Who can restate the proverb in other words?

Reflective Questions
What did you feel after reading the proverb?

What surprised you in the proverb?

What was your first impression of the proverb? Did you feel agreement, disagreement, understanding, confusion, other emotions?

What image did the proverb create in your mind?

Interpretive Questions

What do you think the proverb means?

What kind of person would repeat this proverb?

In what kind of situation would this proverb be repeated?

What does this proverb suggest about the views of some habitants of Senegal?

If you grew up hearing this proverb often, how might it affect your views?

Do you think this proverb could be interpreted in more than one way?

How might different people interpret this proverb differently?

Decisional Questions

How might your concept of society be different from that of the people whose culture teaches this proverb?

What are some ways in which you act to please society?

What significance could this proverb have for your life?

What did you learn about the culture in which the proverb originated?

Based on the proverb, what behaviors might help you if you moved to Senegal and wanted to be accepted in Senegalese society?

What behaviors might be unacceptable in Senegalese society?

What might be the consequences of unacceptable behavior?

As discussion is drawing to a close, I conclude, "We get information about different cultures in different ways. You have learned a lot about Senegal already just from discussing this proverb. Now we can read from some other sources and see if what we read about Senegal confirms the impression we got from the proverb."

I use proverbs from Senegal because I am most familiar with them, but all African countries have oral traditions that include proverbs. The following list of proverbs from Senegal illustrates the many different kinds of cultural information that can be found in proverbs. (The translations from the Wolof are my own, with emphasis on the literal to retain some of the original language effect.) Any one of these proverbs would be suitable for lessons using the "guided conversations" approach.

Senegalese Proverbs

Standing on tiptoe may make you taller, but when your feet tire you'll be the same height you always are.

If ten people dig a hole and ten others fill it up, there will be a lot of dust flying but no hole.

To curtsey to someone does not prevent you from carrying your knees with you when you go on your way.

It's not because you have shaken the tree that the fruit has fallen, but because it was ripe.

Slowly, slowly catches the monkey on the plains.

News doesn't have legs, but it can cross rivers.

A rude tongue is a small weapon.

Hide yourself and say, "I see no one," but don't say, "No one sees me."

One who is patient will smile.

Life is not couscous, so find something to make it easier to swallow.

Help is found in one's own hands.

Do what you can, say what you know, and when you go to bed, you'll sleep.

Respect is more valuable than beauty.

People are their own best remedies.

For further information, you might want to check Ruth Finnegan's *Oral Literature in Africa* (Clarendon Press, 1979) or *African Proverbs* by Wolf and Charlotte Leslau (Peter Pauper Press, 1962).

Deborah Fredo, Amherst, Massachusetts

Teaching Style with Style

Imagine that you've just walked into a room filled with strangers. How do you decide with whom to start up a conversation? Is your eye more likely to be caught by someone who looks sporty, frilly, sophisticated, or unconventional? Are you drawn more to a person with a jaunty air, or to someone who appears earnest and sincere?

Or suppose that you're choosing a recording to play on your stereo. Do you reach for Mozart, Brahms, or Stravinsky? Perhaps lively dance music is your most frequent choice. Or is your preference jazz, blues, or rock?

These examples illustrate briefly the individuality of style. But just what is style? How do you identify it? What makes you prefer one style to another? Discussion of these and other questions about style can lead your students to a better understanding of literature—of how an author's unique perspective and personality work together to engage the reader's response. Give your students a chance to study style in a six- or seven-day unit presented after the class has studied several distinctly different authors and their works.

Day One

If you like, you can open your first class session just as I opened this article. If you prefer to use a different example, ask your students to think about what they are wearing. "How do you choose your clothes?" "Is there a certain 'look'—whether casual, dressy, or zany—that you think of as *you*?" "Have you ever thought to yourself about a particular piece of clothing, 'That just wouldn't match my personality'?" Point out that personal style can be reflected even in such a simple matter as selecting one color or fabric over another.

Next, ask a volunteer to look up the word *style* in the dictionary and to read the definition aloud to the class. Ask students to provide examples of how they ordinarily use the word *style* in conversation. Pose questions such as: "How is *style* similar to and different from *class, flair,* or *pizzazz*?" "What does it mean when you say someone *has style*?" " . . . when you say someone is *stylish*?" "What does the term *stylized* mean?" "What do we mean by saying someone dresses in a Victorian style?"

Following this introductory discussion, I use four reproductions of paintings of bridges to illustrate diversity of style in works of art. (The reproductions I use are Albert Marquet's "The Pont Neuf," Claude Monet's "Waterloo Bridge," a Chinese painting by an unknown artist titled "Bijutsu/Sha/Scala," and Joseph Skalla's modern interpretation, "The Brooklyn Bridge.") For this part of the lesson, you can use any four reproductions depicting the same subject. As you present the four examples, encourage your students to notice how shape and line, roughness or slickness of texture, perspective, and other elements express the artist's style and personal feeling about the subject. Point out, too, that the style of any work is partly the result of the time, place, and culture.

Use the remaining time to suggest and elicit from students examples of style in language—for example, formal styles such as those used in business letters and law, and informal styles such as those used in advertising slogans, slang, bumperstickers, and T-shirts.

Day Two

Plan to spend the first part of this class period in discussion and the second part in explaining a group writing assignment.

Start the class period by distributing copies of short, unlabeled passages from works studied in class. First ask students to identify the author of each passage and then ask them what clues might help them to identify the author if they were familiar with his or her style but had not read that particular work. For instance, Hemingway might be identified by short sentences, or Poe by his use of description. Finally, explore with students how the styles of the sample works differ, comparing and contrasting the following elements: diction (individual word choice), syntax (sentence arrangement and variety), and imagery (figurative language). With more advanced classes, you may also want to discuss such techniques as alliteration, assonance, and consonance.

Another way to provoke discussion is to copy part or all of one of the passages onto the chalkboard, changing the structure of several sentences and substituting synonyms for key words and different metaphors for figures of speech. Then let students decide how the style of the passage is affected by the changes.

Before the end of the class period, give instructions for the writing assignment on which students will spend the next two days. Divide the class into groups of four or five, hand out copies of a simple tale—"The Little Red Hen" works well, as would a fable—and explain that each group will be assigned an author previously studied and will rewrite the tale in the style of that author. The identity of the author assigned to the group will be known only to the members of that group. After the rewriting is completed, a member of the group will read the story aloud and the rest of the class will try to identify the author by the style of writing. Assign each group an author and let students use the remaining time in the period to read over the original tale. (Don't worry if you have to assign the same author to two different groups. That can make for some interesting results, too.)

Days Three, Four, and Maybe Five

While students write, all you need worry about is your duty as a consultant. Your message should be: decide on the most important stylistic features of your author and try to remain faithful to his or her style. If some groups need a third day for writing, you can encourage the others to use the time to plan the dramatic presentation of their story. Groups with more time may want to enhance the reading with multiple readers, simple costumes, or even backdrops and props.

The Last Day or Two

When all groups have finished writing, they are ready to take turns presenting their versions to the rest of the class. After each reading, the members of the group are responsible for fielding guesses as to the author the group was imitating and for discussing elements of his or her style.

Follow-Up

Following the presentations and readings, you might want to give your students a list of quotations on writing style. Such a list, possibly including the quotations listed below, could be used to stimulate further discussion or could serve as the basis for an expository writing.

> "The style is the man himself." (de Buffon, *Discourse*)
>
> "Prose is architecture not interior decoration." (Ernest Hemingway, *Death in the Afternoon*)
>
> " . . . the pattern appeals to our aesthetic sense, it causes us to see the book as a whole." (E. M. Forster, *Aspects of the Novel*)
>
> "He who has nothing to assert has no style and can have none: he who has something to assert will go as far in power of style as its momentousness and his conviction will carry him." (George Bernard Shaw, introduction to *Man and Superman*)
>
> "Style is the dress of thought. . . ." (Rev. Samuel Wesley, *An Epistle to a Friend Concerning Poetry*)
>
> "Proper words in proper places, make the true definition of style." (Jonathan Swift, *Letter to a Young Clergyman*)
>
> "In the greatest art, one is always aware of things that cannot be said . . . , of the contradiction between expression and the presence

of the inexpressible. Stylistic devices are also techniques of avoidance. The most potent elements in a work of art are, often, its silences." (Susan Sontag, "On Style" in *Against Interpretation*)

As the year progresses, keep your students' awareness of literary style alive and growing by remembering to note parallels and contrasts in style among the authors on your expanding list.

Beverly Haley, Fort Morgan, Colorado

The Elegy: A Comparative Approach for Students of High Ability

Able students may find W. H. Auden's "In Memory of W. B. Yeats" a highly rewarding poem in itself, richly varied in structure, tone, and ideas. Capable students, however, profit even more from studying this poem in combination with Shelley's "Adonais" or Milton's "Lycidas," both elegies in the pastoral tradition. Through such a comparative approach, Auden's poem provides a natural introduction to many aspects of modern poetry, to the elegy in its various forms, and to stimulating considerations about the nature of poetry and the poet's place in society.

Assign the two poems for independent reading and for group analysis, with students working in groups of four or five. The groups are first to explicate each poem and then to list basic differences in the ways the poets handle their subject. Absolutely no discussion of conventions of the pastoral elegy should precede this independent investigation, though you should be available to help clarify troublesome passages and allusions, to play recordings of each poem, and to raise questions that stimulate more penetrating analysis. Given the length and complexity of these poems, students will probably need two class periods to complete their lists.

After sharing their independent observations of the Auden poem and "Adonais," alert students were quick to offer such comments as these:

> Auden's poem seems almost deliberately cold and objective, while Shelley makes the reader feel the world has come to an end because the poet has died. Shelley digresses, but Auden sticks closely to his subject all the way through.

> Auden actually brings out some of Yeats's personal faults.

> Shelley makes his subject seem almost too good for this world.

> The language in these poems is certainly different! Auden's poem sounds like a conversation except for the last section, while Shelley's is much more formal and eloquent.

> Auden seems most concerned about the immortality of Yeats's poetry, Shelley about the immortality of the man.

At no time, of course, should comparison of the two poems contribute to setting up one as superior to the other. What should become evident is that each poet wrote in different times and circumstances, for different purposes and effects.

Through such interchange and reexamination of specific passages in the two poems, the class should inductively arrive at an awareness of the traditional conventions of the pastoral elegy used by Shelley. Then, with a shock of discovery, they should return to Auden's poem to perceive that he has deliberately refuted these pastoral conventions. By writing an "anti-elegy," he has demonstrated what he believes a true elegy should be. In section one, for example, students should notice how Auden has undercut the impact of personal grief by showing the "cold" indifference of man and nature to the physical death of a human being—albeit a famous one. In section two they should note that he mentions the deficiencies of the dead man and thereby makes him more convincingly human. Honoring a man in spite of his faults is surely a higher tribute than the hyperbolic praise that the pastoral elegy conventionally employs. In section three, a tightly rhymed litany in the rhythm of "Jack and Jill," students should perceive Auden's central theme that while "poetry makes nothing happen," great poetry can make people of a given society more sensitive, thoughtful, and aware, and perhaps more capable of preventing war and social oppression such as that which threatened Europe in 1939, the year of Yeats's death.

At this stage of discussion you might suggest that Auden's poem exhibits a number of characteristics that mark it as a "modern" poem, significantly different from works by Victorian or Romantic poets. Like other poems in the modern tradition, it undercuts emotion through the use of understatement and specific, actually technical, language. It also uses such blunt language and imagery as "guts of the living" and the metaphor of political insurrection for a man's death. Further, as is characteristic of twentieth-century poetry, it exhibits several shifts in tone and point of view, corresponding to shifts in idea, rather than maintaining a uniform tone and pattern. Above all, Auden has refused to pretend to a personal grief he does not feel or, as Shakespeare would say, have his tribute "belied with false compare."

Other modern elegies and "anti-elegies" could be profitably read and compared: Peter Viereck's "Poet" (which closely parallels Auden's approach), Theodore Roethke's "Elegy for Jane," Richard Wilbur's "To An American Poet Just Dead," and Dylan Thomas's "A Refusal to Mourn the Death of a Child by Fire." A broader survey of the elegy might include Ben Jonson's "On My First Son," William Wordsworth's "Lucy" poems, Edna St. Vincent Millay's "Elegy," and, if it has not been handled before, Walt Whitman's "When Lilacs Last in the Dooryard Bloomed."

Growing naturally from a study of Auden's poem could also come considerations about the nature of poetry and the poet's place in society. Auden has made claims for poetry, yet he placed limitations on what it can do, establishing a point of view that leads to a number of other poems defining or commenting on poetry: Archibald MacLeish's "Ars Poetica," Marianne Moore's "Poetry," Dylan Thomas's "In My Craft and Sullen Art," Wallace Stevens's "Of Modern Poetry," and Carl Sandburg's "Ten Definitions of Poetry." All of these investigations, however, should ultimately lead back to Auden's poem, enforcing his assertion that, while individuals die and worlds crumble, the written word survives.

Gladys V. Veidemanis, North High School, Oshkosh, Wisconsin

"The Hollow Men": The Video

In this "postliterate" age of disk, tube, and cassette, the prospect of teaching serious literature to young people is at times daunting. Raised on the ritual formulas of TV sitcoms, the apparently mindless lyrics of rock music, and the quick cuts and breakneck pace of much contemporary film, how can adolescents be expected to give to literature the passionate attention we believe it requires, to use their minds to participate fully in the literary experience?

But wait . . . perhaps it's possible that our students are learning something from the electronic media that they can use to their advantage in reading literature—especially modern literature, which is often non-linear and initially baffling even to experienced readers. I was struck by this possibility while watching a rock video in which the words of the song were paralleled with an apparently unconnected series of images.

A connection existed, however, between the associations created by the images, a connection primarily of mood and emotion. Rock lyrics lend themselves to this kind of presentation, since the music is always there to provide continuity. As Ric Ocasek of the Cars stated, "My lyrics are designed to set up images. Or a mood. Or a transformation from one thing to another. A vision. A light painting. . . . A bunch of manipulated contradictions. . . ."

This same process, of course, defines a great deal of modern poetry. Although poetry does not *fix* the images for the reader (fortunately), young viewers of rock video, although they may not realize it, understand the patterning of images quite well. I capitalize on this understanding when I teach modern poetry; for example, a poem such as "The Hollow Men" by T. S. Eliot.

Before I play a tape of the poem read by Eliot to a class of seniors, I tell them that Eliot is commenting on modern life in much the same way as some of their favorite lyricists do. I ask them to concentrate on the words of the poem as it is read and to imagine that they will be making a video of the poem. They will choose images for the screen that communicate the essential atmosphere and emotion of the poem. Immediately after hearing the tape, each student is to write for fifteen minutes describing as much of his or her video as possible given the time constraints. Students are to restrict their descriptions to what the viewer will *see*.

Some of my students' screen images were predictable: "straw dummies leaning together on the floor of a dark cellar. Some of the stuffing has come out. . . ." But even those students who used images taken directly from the poem showed a strong sense of the visual: "a large desert sprinkled liberally with cactus. Way off in the distance is a long dark line. . . . As the line and the camera get closer we see that the line consists of human shaped figures. They are dark with long hair and their lips are moving." Or: "stuffed dummies whispering . . . to each other in a vast field. Then . . . flashes to rats in the cellar. Next, you are in the fire of the underworld. It is like ancient Greece and there are people without eyes. . . . A dark desert with a hand with bugs crawling on it in the sand." Many students went further and created their own images: "men stepping out of a subway after what appears to be a post-holocaust situation." Or: "Break to an ordinary man lying awake in bed, dreaming of hell. . . ."

After students have written for fifteen minutes, I list as many of their images as possible on the board. We discuss various ways of categorizing the images, beginning with "positive" and "negative." It doesn't take long for the students to see patterns of death and life, despair and hope, sterility and fertility in their representations. At this point I tell them that they have understood the poem on one essential level, and now they should go back to the text and see how the poet has structured the emotions and ideas. As we work together with the text, they come to realize that Eliot is working within a context that the images only suggest. By responding to the vision, students find a way into the poem. They realize that poetry isn't all that different from other aspects of their experience, and they gain confidence in themselves as readers.

Suzanne Howell, Carbondale, Illinois

"Not Getting Along": A Thematic Literature Unit

Paula Danziger's novel *It's an Aardvark-Eat-Turtle World* (Delacorte Press, 1985) provides the perfect stepping-off point for a thematic literature unit focused on relationship under stress, a unit I call "Not Getting Along." A sequel to *The Divorce Express* (Dell, 1986), *It's an Aardvark-Eat-Turtle World* is the story of Rosie, the narrator, and her best friend, Phoebe, both fourteen. Rosie is the daughter of a black father and a white mother who sometime before the beginning of the novel have gotten a divorce. Her father has remarried and moved away, and she lives with her mother. Phoebe is also the daughter of divorced parents. Her mother has remarried and she lives with her father, who has resigned his well-paying job to become a painter. As the novel starts, Rosie's mother and Phoebe's father have decided to live together and have, thus, created a new four-member family. Shortly after the start of the novel, they move into a rather small, rather run-down house.

The rest of the novel deals with the stresses that these new relations place on the friendship between the two girls and on their relations with their parents and step-parents. Phoebe, in fact, leaves the new family to live with her mother and pompous step-father. And Rosie falls in love with a step-cousin of Phoebe's Jason. The story is told in Danziger's breezy, joking style. It is easy and fast reading, and Rosie is a good choice as narrator because she sees humor and irony even in painful situations such as the temporary breakdown of her new family, her embarrassment when her mother and Phoebe's father kiss, and her separation from Jason. In other words, as usual, Danziger treats serious subjects in a light-hearted way.

It's an Aardvark-Eat-Turtle World is just one of the components of this unit, which is intended for seventh grade classes and selected sixth or eighth grade classes. "Not Getting Along" deals specifically with teenagers' problems with parents, with best friends of the same sex, and with friends of the opposite sex. During the course of study, students also look in an informal way at the first-person narrative technique and at how authors use dialogue.

First, the class is divided into four groups. Since at the age of twelve or thirteen, boys and girls, in most cases, work best in groups of the same sex, there are two groups of boys and two of girls. The young adult novels that these students will read are:

Group I: Girls—*It's an Aardvark-Eat-Turtle World*

Group II: Girls—*Are You There, God? It's Me, Margaret* by Judy Blume (Dell, 1986)

Group III: Boys—*Rabbit Ears* by Robert Montgomery (New American Library, 1985)

Group IV: Boys—*Chernowitz!* by Fran Arrick (New American Library, 1983)

The members of each group are asked to read over a period of several days the novel assigned to that group. Some reading will take place in class, especially on the first day of the unit, but most of it will be carried on outside of class. For this reason, students will be asked to keep readers' journals. As soon as the reading for that day has been completed, students will write down the responses that they have had to the characters and events. John W. Swope ("Journals: Capturing Students' Responses to Literature," *Virginia English Bulletin,* Winter 1985, pp. 35–41) suggests this device as a means of bridging the time gap between reading at home and discussing in class a day later.

Students in each group will be asked to consider how and how well the teenagers in the novel deal with their problems with other teenagers and with their parents. At the same time, they will also be asked to consider how and how well the adults in the novel deal with their problems with other people. Finally, students will be asked to compare the success of the teenagers' coping with that of the adults. These topics will be the foci of the daily group discussions.

As students read, they will also be asked to project how the novels will turn out. In each of these novels, there are key points at which projections can be made about future events. For example, in *It's an Aardvark-Eat-Turtle World,* at the point when Phoebe has left and Rosie is separated from Jason, students will be asked to look at the teenager-teenager, teenager-parent, and adult-adult relations and project how they will turn out.

Once the students in each group have finished reading the novel and have discussed the various relationships and ways of coping with problems that are present in that novel, the class as a whole will look at the three problem areas as revealed in their novels and in their own experiences. The students will identify the nature of the problems and successful and unsuccessful ways of coping with them. They will also discuss how well teenagers cope with the problems compared to how well adults cope.

Although teenagers in the middle school grades are mostly interested in literature as a way of testing themselves and their values, as Robert Carlsen states in *Books and the Teenage Reader* (Harper and Row, 1980), students of this age can begin to understand how authors do what they do. The young adult novel is an excellent means for introducing students to the art of literature. This unit asks the students to look at two aspects of the craft of literature in a way they can understand.

First, since all four novels are first-person narratives, each group will be asked to think about how that narrator tells the story. In their groups, they will be asked to look at this aspect of their novel, using the following as a guide:

1. —————— is telling the story. Can you find any places where he/she may be giving his/her own views and not telling the full story? What makes you think so?

2. Suppose —————— (another teenage character) had told the story. How might the novel have been different?

3. Pick an important scene and rewrite it as —————— (that same other character) might tell it. Keep the main facts the same, but let the rest of it be as —————— would have seen and told what happened.

When the groups have finished their consideration and writing, each group will present its ideas and rewritten scene to the whole class.

In addition to being a first-person narrative, each of these novels uses a good deal of dialogue to tell the story and to reveal the characters. Consequently, each group will be asked, as a final project, to carry out the following activities:

1. Listen to your friends. What do they say? How do they say it? Spend a day or two listening and watching instead of being a part of the talking. The lunch table, the locker room, and the school bus are all good places to listen. Write down what you can remember. Then, in your group, share your dialogues by reading them aloud. Consider how real people sound when they're talking naturally.

2. Read aloud some scenes from your novel that have a lot of dialogue. Did the author get the sound of real people talking? What are the differences? the similarities?

3. Look for a fairly important happening in the book that you are told about but don't actually watch happening. You are going to write the missing scene. First, notice how the author described other important happenings in the book. Then write the missing scene, giving the words of the characters and describing their actions.

These activities may not be easy for some students, but they will learn from them a bit about what authors do to create novels. These "writing from literature" activities will challenge them to think about what they've read and to go beyond the book to see its relation to themselves. Done in a group and with the help of the teacher, such activities will help students begin to see literature as a means to understand themselves and others.

Robert Small, Jr., Virginia Polytechnic Institute and State University, Blacksburg, Virginia

Poetry Filmstrips

After the students in my advanced-placement senior English class demonstrated their mastery of research paper skills, I wanted to find a more creative project that would use research skills yet take students beyond a paper assignment. The idea of letting students make filmstrips came to me from a seminar on teaching gifted students. As a result, I developed the "poetry filmstrip project," in which students work in pairs or small groups to create a critical biography of a poet in filmstrip form. This project takes six weeks: the completed filmstrips are shown to the class and, to the pride of the creators, become a permanent part of our English department film library.

To complete this project, each pair or group of students will need the use of a 35mm camera for the photographing of the slides and the use of a cassette tape recorder for the recording of the commentary accompanying the filmstrip. (If obtaining such equipment in quantity is a problem, the project can still be accomplished as long as you can beg or borrow *one* camera and *one* tape recorder. A schedule for the use of the equipment is then essential for assuring all students enough time for photographing slides and for tape recording commentaries.)

Here is the handout sheet of instructions and guidelines I give my students:

Poetry Filmstrip Project

You and your partner or group will be preparing in filmstrip form a critical biography of a poet. You will need to research and present a summary of the poet's life and work, including the place and date of the poet's birth, details of his or her education, influences on the poet's writing, prizes received, and discussion of his or her most important poems, touching on major themes and symbols as well as other pertinent characteristics of the poet's style. Select one poet from the following list, or choose a poet not on this list, subject to my approval. (If you choose a more contemporary poet, make sure that enough criticism has been written about the poet and his or her work to make your research possible.)

William Blake	John Donne
Dante Gabriel Rossetti	Ben Jonson
Samuel Taylor Coleridge	Percy Bysshe Shelley
Robert Browning	Alfred, Lord Tennyson
John Keats	William Wordsworth
Matthew Arnold	Emily Dickinson
W. B. Yeats	Wilfred Owen

T. S. Eliot	Dylan Thomas
e. e. cummings	A. E. Housman
W. H. Auden	William Carlos Williams
Walt Whitman	Langston Hughes
Robert Graves	Philip Larkin
Ted Hughes	Gwendolyn Brooks
Sylvia Plath	

Consult any and all possible sources of information on your poet—books, magazines, literary criticism, the encyclopedia, and whatever else you can find. To locate pictures of the poet and his or her environs to photograph for the filmstrip, consult books and magazines and use the world around you— the world of nature, the city or wherever your poet went for inspiration. Use your imagination in choosing images to match your commentary.

Your spoken commentary should be at least twenty minutes long, which will make the filmstrip about fifty frames in length (requiring two rolls of film). You might imagine that you have been commissioned by an educational publishing company to prepare something for high school English classrooms; make your commentary scholarly and yet clear and easy to understand.

If you use literary criticism, remember to include a bibliography of your sources at the end of your filmstrip. Please put everything into your own words; do not quote straight from the source.

These are the basic steps to follow:

1. Decide on a poet.

2. To get a sense for the poet's work, find out which two or three poems are considered the best of his or her work. (I can help you get started here.)

3. Read through each poem several times and discuss each with your partner or the members of your group.

4. Begin your research, taking thorough notes. Start with basic information about the poet's life, move on to his or her work, and finally focus on two or three poems that best demonstrate the poet's talent and insight. If these poems are too long to be

included in their entirety in the commentary, you may want
to select and read aloud an excerpt from each.

5. With your partner or the members of your group, decide on
    the organization of your material and begin writing the com-
    mentary. Don't begin to gather visual material until you have
    a rough draft of the commentary.

6. Before you begin to take photographs, have an idea of the
    types of images you will want to accompany the different
    parts of your commentary. You must take your photographs
    in the actual sequence in which you want them to be viewed.
    Take about fifty photographs.

7. Allow two weeks for the developing of the film. *Tell the photo
    processor to develop your prints as for slides but not to cut
    the film and not to mount it into slides.* This is very important.
    If your photographs are cut apart, you have no filmstrip!

8. Once your developed filmstrip has been returned, edit and
    polish the commentary to match the frames of the filmstrip.
    On the copy of the commentary, indicate where a bell or
    buzzer is to be rung to signal the advance of the frame.

9. Type a final, perfect copy of your commentary, indicating
    where each frame will change. This is the "filmstrip
    transcript" that will be stored with your filmstrip in the
    English department archives.

10. Tape-record your commentary. If you are working in a group,
    you could either choose a student with a good speaking voice
    to read the entire commentary, or each group member could
    read a segment. Include the sound of a bell or buzzer to
    indicate where the filmstrip frame should be changed.

Your presentation on the life and work of your chosen poet should now
be ready for presentation to the class.

Peggy Guerin, Huntsville High School, Huntsville, Alabama

Writing Assignment of the Month

Mapping: A Prewriting Technique That Works

Every writer begins by facing a blank page, waiting for ideas and words. Some writers make lists before writing, some work out ideas in their minds, some outline, some doodle—but all writers develop techniques for beginning. Mapping is one such technique. Because it helps writers generate ideas, because it allows them to add or delete material readily, and because it is easily learned, mapping is an extremely useful skill.

What Is a Map?

A map is a graphic representation of a written or oral composition; often it includes only key words. It adds a visual dimension that helps students gain greater control of and fluency in thinking and writing. A map helps students produce and receive information, organize that information, and go on to create a product uniquely their own. Because it teaches students to differentiate among primary, secondary, and tertiary ideas, a map aids composing and comprehending. Mapping can be a prewriting, revising, or postwriting activity, enabling students to organize, compose, and evaluate their writing.

Introducing Mapping

Introduce mapping to students with an everyday topic that allows them to work together to generate an extensive list of related words and ideas. This step does not differ significantly from what is often called brainstorming. With junior high students I have used such topics as sports or soap; with high school students such topics as advertising or the troubles of being seventeen. Writing about a best friend or what-if topics (What if no adults came to school today?) are also good choices.

When students seem to have run out of ideas, we organize the words into categories. At this step students frequently get new ideas and insights as they begin to perceive a structure that can be expanded or contracted depending upon the writer's purpose and intent. The topic *soap*, for example, yielded the following terms and categories:

type	*use*	*color*	*smell*	*texture*
liquid	shower	white	fresh	gritty
powdered	bath	green	lemon	granule
bar	dishes	pink	clean	slippery
	clothes	yellow	herbal	bubbly
	laundry	creamy	bayberry	sudsy
	cleaning	milky	spicy	satiny
	cars	iridescent	outdoorsy	creamy
	lubricant		pine	fluffy
	blowing bubbles		floral	smooth

Next, students arrange these categories and words on a map like the one on page 66, with the controlling topic or idea in a dominant position and the supporting ideas as extensions. A pinwheel shape, however, is only one of the many configurations that will develop. Again, new ideas often emerge during mapping and additions and deletions should be encouraged. At this step, mapping encourages interaction among students, and these interchanges help to prepare students to write their own essays later on.

Based on our map, we work out a topic sentence as a group and draft a first paragraph together before students take off on their own to complete their drafts. We revise these in small groups, and read some to the class and show others on the overhead projector.

After an introduction to mapping, students typically go on to create more individualistic maps. Older students develop relatively sophisticated ones (interlocking triangles, concentric circles, ladders) that help them structure their writing and shape it for special purposes and audiences. Mapping in a sense provides its own outline—each category inviting development with explanation, definition, classification, example, narration, comparison.

Mapping a More Complicated Assignment

Mapping a short story or essay before writing about it helps students discern how an author has structured ideas. The example on page 67 illustrates how a fifteen-year-old sophomore was able to show parallels between Chaucer's "Knight's Tale" and his "Miller's Tale"—first by mapping, then in writing a first draft of a comparison paper. Clearly, the

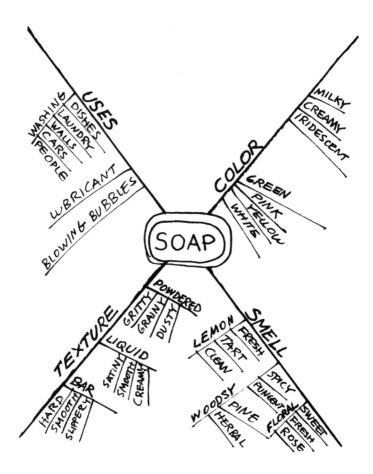

mapping technique assisted this student in writing a draft that both analyzes and synthesizes the structures of the two tales.

A Comparison of the Knight's Tale and the Miller's Tale

After the knight finished his beautiful (and overlong) tale, everyone agreed it was noble. The drunken miller, however, thought he could match any tale of the knight's. At first, the two tales seem to be totally opposite, but after a closer look one can find many similarities.

Both tales involve a love triangle, where two men seek the love of the same woman and fight for her. In "The Knight's Tale" the characters are Palamon, Arcite, and Emily. In "The Miller's Tale" the characters are

Absalom, Nicholas, and Alison. The knight's triangle is very pure and romantic. The miller's triangle is somewhat raunchier; Nicholas, for example, had already won Alison while Absalom was still begging for her love.

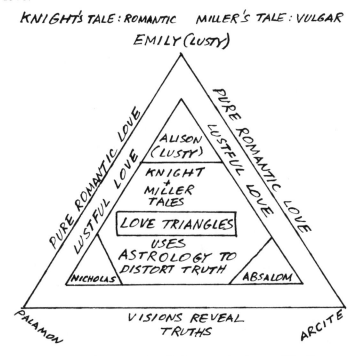

Visions are used in both tales. Palamon, Arcite, and Emily pray to the gods in an effort to guide their destiny, and Emily sees a vision of the goddess Diana. In the miller's tale visions are mocked. Nicholas also uses visions in an effort to guide his destiny—or his and Alison's. He pretends to have seen a vision from the gods, telling him a great flood is coming, to trick the carpenter into hiding in a barrel.

Destiny solved the differences between Palamon and Arcite. Both men won, even though Arcite died. He won Emily's hand in marriage and then had an accident. As he lay dying, he gave Emily to Palamon. So it was in the miller's tale; everyone was "rewarded" so to speak: foolish Absalom with a misplaced kiss, over-confident Nicholas with a severely burned bottom, and the anxious carpenter with a broken arm.

The miller took almost every detail of the knight's tale and twisted it into something vulgar so that the stories seem to be very dissimilar.

However, after careful scrutiny, many likenesses can be found. As a matter of fact, both stories parallel each other.

Conclusion

Mapping enhances verbal thinking because it provides a visual/spatial perspective, allowing poorer writers to generate and shape ideas with greater ease and assisting more sophisticated writers with analysis and synthesis. Mapping seems to be effective because it combines what Susanne Langer called the discursive (speaking, listening, reading, and writing) with the presentational (art, music, dance, and sculpture)—two basic ways we symbolize experience. By using both the verbal and the spatial modes of thinking, mapping takes full advantage of the symbolic process.

If we want students to generate words easily, if we want them to organize their essays or stories efficiently, if we want them to write coherently, then mapping is one of the skills we will teach. As a prewriting activity it helps students begin, as a shaping activity it helps them form their ideas, as a holistic activity it helps them to synthesize ideas. Because mapping takes advantage of our verbal and visual abilities, it adds a new dimension and power to all language activities, especially writing.

Owen Boyle, Assistant Director, Bay Area Writing Project

Writing to Learn across the Curriculum

One of the most promising movements in education today is "writing across the curriculum" or, more recently and more accurately, "writing to learn." An outgrowth of the focus on writing as process rather than product, it restores to writing a function it naturally has in life and in education. Rather than a mere school exercise, or even an act of communication, writing becomes an instrument of thinking and learning in itself. Youngsters who are taught how to use writing to make sense of new material, to sort out and classify what they are learning *as they are learning it,* to speculate and react, to integrate the new language of the subject matter with their own language, are being taught—not *what* to think but *how* to go about thinking.

Using writing to learn is not a complicated matter for teachers or students. Neither is it an expensive innovation; it is as cheap as paper and pen. Teachers who wish to use writing as a means of learning in their disciplines need not be writing teachers or authorities on grammar. What is needed is a subtle turning around by the teacher to look in another direction—toward the process of thinking and learning rather than at the products.

Practice on Yourself

How can a teacher begin to use writing to learn? First, try it yourself with a speculative journal. Choose something to read; whether you know it well or not at all is immaterial. Find at least an hour to read, paper and pen in hand. As you read, stop frequently to write. Do not take notes or copy down the text. Rather, write what comes to mind: questions, reactions, problems, memories.

After a half hour, look back over what you have written. You will discover that you have noted more details, made more associations, observed more about the thought of the selection, and done more real thinking than you ordinarily do when you read. If the material was new, maybe even difficult, you will see a gradual figuring out of how to go about reading the material and perhaps a good many questions. Gradually you will observe increasing commitment to and involvement with the material as you are drawn into it through the active process of writing.

Go on with your reading and writing, observing what your mind is doing with the material as it integrates it with your personal store of knowledge, feelings, and ideas. This is exactly what will happen with your students. Although you will not be concerned with syntax, spelling, or other details of finished compositions since this writing is for you alone, you will discover ideas that could be expanded and elaborated into more formal composition later. So will your students. When they write to learn, writing falls into its place as a tool for learning first and as a means of communication second. You could even go back through your speculative journal and underline the best ideas for future writing or discussion.

This approach can be refined further with a double-entry technique. Draw a line down the center of your page. As you read, jot down in the left column phrases, words, sentences that catch your attention. Just after you have written something on the left, move to the right column and write your responses, questions, comments. As you move through the text, you will notice that this technique causes you to focus on specifics, draws you in close to the text, produces analytical and critical thinking on your part, and draws your attention to matters of style and arrangement. This approach is ideal for math, physics, chemistry, poetry, for any text that calls for close reading and attention to specifics.

Classroom Application

When you introduce writing to learn to students, expect some resistance. "It slows me down," is the common complaint. Yes, it does. That is partly its purpose. Slow down and think about what you are reading. Develop some ideas of your own rather than merely digesting the ideas in the text to be returned to the teacher on the test. I have found that the most capable students are most likely to object at first, simply because they already know how to make A's and see no need to do anything differently. But it is these students who benefit most from the approach and who, in the end, appreciate it most deeply. Less capable students often accept the approach more readily, for it means they will always have something to contribute to class—their questions and their reactions.

Now, how are you to use the writing students have done in speculative or double-entry notebooks? If too much emphasis is put upon grading or evaluating the writing itself, it will soon turn into a product rather than a process, and we will be back in the same dead end. Better that it be looked at first for quantity and commitment and then integrated into classroom activities through conversation in small groups. Ask at the beginning of class for a half-sheet of paper on which students record how many pages they have written on the assigned reading, how many pages they have read, and at least one good question or insight from their writing. I group students who are at the same point in their reading, and they discuss the questions and ideas they have recorded. I circulate among the groups, listening to the discussion and adding information or comments from time to time. Talking about what one has read and written is absolutely vital; it means that every student makes the language of the subject at hand a part of his or her personal language—something that seldom happens in teacher lectures or large class "discussions" where a few students dominate. Later, when the small groups summarize their discussion for the whole class, other gains are made: restatement of ideas, selection and ordering, and the act of speaking to a larger group in a nonthreatening situation.

What other uses can be made of the writing? Last semester I asked advanced placement students to find in their speculative writing from the unit on medieval literature five questions that interested them, to rank those five, and to take the top question as a personal I-search (Macrorie's term—a rebuttal to *re*search) to be presented as a paper and a class report telling where they looked, what they found, and what they thought of what they found. The assignment resulted in twenty-four lively, thoughtful searches into psychology, social history, theology, philosophy, and even historiography—fields that most of my students had not known existed—and into interviews with an assortment of people and reading in several large libraries. I have never before had students listen with such interest to the presentations of their peers, and the method was much closer to that of true research rather than the patch work that often goes by the name. And, of course, students wrote speculative and double-entry logs as they did their research, the double-entry technique being especially suited since it records passage and response at the same time and in the same place. I ask younger or less capable students to talk in groups from their writing-to-learn notebooks and then to write informal summaries of their impressions. These are shared in writing groups, revised and edited, and put into a class anthology of commentary on a story or book or unit of study.

Finally, most students reread their logs before tests or in-class essays. Of course, they also enjoy looking back later to see how they responded to a book when first meeting it. One junior buys a notebook the same size as the book she is reading "so I can put it right beside the book on my shelf." She likes to think about her grandchildren reading her notebook some day and wonders if they will read the same books and what they will think of her 1980's ideas.

Student Reactions

What happens when a student uses writing to learn about new subject matter? Let a few high school juniors respond to that question.

> At first I didn't know how to begin . . . but after I experimented with the process I found that I understood what I read much better and . . . could respond . . . much better and in more detail.

I asked a lot of questions—the unanswerable type.

I doubt that I would have understood [the book] without the benefit of writing.

I don't think I could have done without a journal. There were just too many things that had to come out of myself and not necessarily out of the book.

Dixie Dellinger, Burns Senior High School, Lawndale, North Carolina

The Clothesline

What we wear is an important consideration for most of us. Whether we dress to express our flamboyant selves or hope that our clothes—like protective coloration—will protect us in uncomfortable situations, we choose our clothing with care. Perhaps the young are most susceptible to fashion's dictates; at any rate, Madison Avenue makes special appeals to the teenage market. The following writing assignments offer students an opportunity to explore the puzzling effects of clothes in our lives and in literature.

1. Ask students to share an experience or anecdote that reveals the importance of a specific article of clothing in their lives. As a first step, ask students to share their ideas orally in small groups. After students have talked about their experiences and heard about the experiences of others in the class, they are better equipped to present their own experience or anecdote as a personal essay or narrative.

2. Assign one or more short stories in which an article of clothing has special significance in revealing the traits or personality of a particular character (for example, the fur piece in Katherine Mansfield's "Miss Brill"). Have students prepare a written analysis of why clothing is so important to the character. The narrow focus of this assignment helps students know what elements to discuss.

3. Have students write a character sketch in which details of clothing are central to the creation of character.

4. Ask students to write a one-paragraph lost-and-found notice for an article of clothing they are wearing. Accurate identification of the article from this description is essential. Shoes are a particularly

successful choice since so many students will be wearing running shoes with distinctive markings. Share these descriptions aloud, asking the class to identify the wearer of each item described.

5. Ask students to write a dialogue in which two teens talk about why they "must have" a particular item of clothing that they cannot afford. Encourage them to make the dialogue express the values of the speakers. As an alternate assignment, students may write a dialogue between a teen and a parent in which the teen argues for the purchase and the parent counters.

6. Cut small pictures of people from magazines like *Time* and *Newsweek* and paste them on file cards. Choose authors, executives, criminals, government officials, and foreign dignitaries, but avoid pictures that students would easily identify, such as Geraldine Ferraro or Alan Alda. I also avoid pictures from ads because professional models tend to look "fake." Ask each student to pick a card and to write a description of the person shown, basing the details solely on deductions made from the person's appearance. The assignment provokes a lively follow-up discussion since students discover how our attitudes toward people are influenced by their dress and physical appearance.

L. D. Groski, LaRoche College, Pittsburgh, Pennsylvania, and Shirley S. Stevens, Quaker Valley High School, Leetsdale, Pennsylvania

Bubblegum Flowers

The first year that I taught tenth-grade composition, my students rebelled halfway through the semester. How, they demanded, could I expect them to write vivid descriptions of *ordinary* objects? I turned to art for help in showing students the importance of the artist's—or writer's—perspective: no matter what the object is, the manner in which it is perceived and portrayed can render it exciting. In developing a new unit, I selected Georgia O'Keeffe as the focus because I knew the class would enjoy her paintings, would appreciate her memoirs, and would find Joan Didion's essay on O'Keeffe in *The White Album* (Washington Square Press, 1979) an accessible model for future writing.

I began by asking my pupils to bring in a fresh flower or two the next day. I also brought in a bunch of daffodils and cut out a number of photographs of flowers from magazines. I looked for the tritest pictures possible—a rose with dewdrops, a huge sunflower, a bright red tulip.

The next day I asked each student to choose one flower, either a real one or a photograph, and to write a paragraph about it, describing it as carefully as possible. After fifteen minutes, I told everyone to stop and called on several students to read their paragraphs aloud. Although the descriptions tended to be stilted and full of clichés, I made no comments. Instead, I walked to a slide projector in the back of the room and showed students several slides of O'Keeffe's flower paintings. I told the class a little about O'Keeffe and then selected one slide for them to describe. (Once I used reproductions instead of slides; this took longer, but it worked well, too.) Again, I allotted fifteen minutes before choosing several students to read their descriptions. The second batch of paragraphs was far more exciting than the first; many students had used unusual similes and metaphors, and one student even compared the flower to the bubblegum underneath her chair!

For the remainder of the period, we compared the two sets of descriptions. Almost everyone agreed that the second batch was superior to the first, and we talked about why examining O'Keeffe's paintings had resulted in better descriptions. Students mentioned selection and emphasis, and we discussed how they might have created interesting descriptions the first time by taking risks and using their imaginations.

On the following day, I read to the students the first few pages of O'Keeffe's memoirs (entitled *Georgia O'Keeffe,* Penguin Books, 1977). The narrative, which is full of light, color, texture, and sound, delighted the students and prompted a discussion of what made it successful. Ultimately, the class decided that the qualities that made her a good painter—her sharp eye and fine sense of humor—also made her an effective writer. As a homework assignment, I asked students to write a one-page description of one of the first events each student could remember from childhood, using what they had learned about prose from O'Keeffe. I also asked them to read Didion's essay on O'Keeffe in *The White Album.*

The next class session opened with a discussion of several students' memories. After savoring these for a few minutes and laughing at particularly outrageous exploits, we moved to Didion's essay, focusing on her use of characterization and details. We also studied the structure of the essay: Was there a thesis about O'Keeffe's personality? What was it? How did Didion prove her point? (One student muttered that Didion did not have to follow a five-paragraph structure, and I brought up some examples of professional artists and writers who have taken risks or liberties with forms *after* they have mastered them.) The rest of the class period was spent in discussion of how students' views of writing had changed during the previous week.

This unit was a valuable diversion for students. The discussion of their own descriptions and of the essay form helped their writing, and they learned something about art as well. But best of all, students learned that the quality of a piece of writing is determined by the writer and not by the subject matter.

Amy Levin, Scarsdale High School, Scarsdale, New York

Writing about Writing

Young writers are often unaware of the struggles and triumphs all writers go through as they compose. By learning how some of their peers cope with the writing process, and by examining the process they themselves use in writing, students can improve their writing and gain confidence.

I usually wait to use this activity until after students have written two or three papers and have done lots of informal writing. On the day when the final draft of a finished paper is due, I collect their work and assign an in-class paper entitled "How I Wrote This Paper." I encourage students to be as specific as possible, including all the details they can remember about working on the paper both at home and in class. I ask them to consider the following questions:

Did you need to write in a special place?

Did you write with the TV on? with music playing? in a quiet atmosphere?

Did you use a particular writing utensil or special paper?

Were there any particular circumstances or techniques that made it easier or more difficult for you to write?

How did you get started?

What did you do if and when you got stuck?

Did you need an outline or notes or freewritings?

How much did you revise?

Did you make more than one draft?

Did you read your work to anyone or talk about it with anyone?

What kind of final editing and polishing did you do?

What was the toughest part of this paper for you?

What was the easiest part?

I allow about twenty minutes for students to write in response to these questions and then ask them to conclude by estimating how much time it took them to write and revise the paper.

Next, I put students into groups of four to read their papers aloud to each other. Once each group member has read his or her paper, I ask students to discuss the questions listed below while one member of the group takes notes. This usually takes another twenty minutes.

1. Were there any similarities among the way group members wrote?
2. Were there major differences among the way group members wrote?
3. Did anyone have an especially interesting or unusual approach to writing?
4. What kinds of circumstances did group members agree made it more difficult to write?
5. What circumstances or techniques would you recommend as making writing easier, faster, or more pleasant?

The final step is to ask each group's "secretary" to make a brief report while I take notes on the board. Usually the reports quite naturally fall into a set of prewriting, writing, revising, and editing strategies, which I organize across the board. This group sharing is often playful as well as instructive as students share their pleasures and pains with the papers they just handed in, offering anecdotes about 3 a.m. inspiration, writer's block, and the emergency trip to the store for a favorite type of ballpoint pen. We conclude by comparing the estimates of writing time, a range that may run from a low of six hours to a high of seventeen for a standard three-page paper.

By the end of this exploration of writing styles, students have some ideas on how to improve the way they write, and also have the assurance that their writing behaviors are normal. An additional bonus for me is that I find it a valuable diagnostic tool. I can see how well my message about the writing process is getting across; but more important, I learn reasons for certain students' writing problems. Problems in a paper, too, can often be explained by examining the process the student used. Knowledge about the amount and kind of work that went into the paper also makes me more understanding as I write comments and assign grades. I can compliment students on strategies they've used that have worked well, or suggest methods that might make their writing even better.

Lois M. Rosen, Flint, Michigan

In Defense of a Challenged Book

Censorship continues to be a rather hot topic across the nation, but many students are oblivious to its potential impact on what they might be able to read in school. This assignment—to select a novel that has at some time suffered attacks (but that is still allowed reading for the district), to discuss possible reasons for the objections, and then to defend the work for classroom use—can open students' eyes to the complexities of the issue. The issue is a sensitive one, and its treatment in the classroom could draw fire in some communities; teachers should use discretion in deciding to use or adapt this assignment with their students.

This assignment first became a part of my college prep composition class when the Colorado Language Arts Society chose a similar topic for its statewide writing contest in 1982. The responses were so thoughtful and varied that I adapted it as a standard part of my course.

The initial reaction of many of my students to a discussion of censorship is "But it never happens here, does it?" so we begin by talking about works that have been challenged in our school and our district, as well as what's going on around the state and country. Students are usually both surprised and intrigued.

Because challenges to classroom materials and methods are on the rise in our district, I believe the prewriting discussion of these issues are vital to more than this assignment's product. Recognizing that some students and/or their parents may be sympathetic to the movement to challenge materials and practices, I counter the typical first—and usually loud—reaction that "those people must be crazy" with an explanation of the honest, protective motives behind most challenges. I encourage students to realize that "those people" are, for the most part, truly concerned parents with a sincere desire to be responsible about what their children are exposed to in required reading. This discussion helps the class approach the assignment with a serious attitude rather than a reactionary one, as they try to identify and understand both the reasons that censors object to certain works and the arguments that might be used in support of those works.

Reproductions of articles on censorship and lists of challenged books spark students' interest and help them make selections to examine in depth. A 1982 article in the September/October issue of *The Bloomsbury Review* entitled "Book Banning: Who Shall Determine the Right to Read?" really starts them thinking.

Within three or four days, each student submits a thesis statement including author and title, potential censor's objections, and their own supporting attitude. This statement is to guide students' work. As students read and plan, their specific objections and arguments may change, but I don't allow students to change their decision as to what work to examine. (Invariably, some students would do so too late to produce a responsible piece of writing.)

After discussion about how to approach the writing, we ordinarily produce several possible patterns of organization for this assignment. Two workable ones appear below.

Organization A:

   I. Introductory paragraph revealing writer's stance
  II. Potential/real objections
 III. Arguments for work's use in schools
 IV. Conclusion

Organization B:

   I. Introductory paragraph previewing objections and revealing writer's stance
  II. Objection-by-objection explanation and refutation
 III. Conclusion

The first pattern seems to work best for students who find the objections reasonable, irrefutable, or unrelated to the real reasons English teachers select the work for the classroom. ("Yes, foul language does exist in *The Catcher in the Rye*.") This includes students who find themselves agreeing with the complaints but supporting the book in spite of the objections. The second format works best for students who want to refute the objections as weak or shortsighted *as* they argue for the novel. ("The language is real, and reality in fiction serves a purpose.")

The products of this assignment have been particularly rewarding. I have kept some copies of the best responses and share them with students judiciously. Insecure writers are sometimes frightened by other students' expertise, and some papers on novels that students are currently scrutinizing are best held until essay are submitted or returned, instead of while work is in progress. Students' creativity has been evident in many of the papers. Students have adopted the voice of a character in the novel, of the author, or of an imaginary English teacher who has received a challenge. Some papers have contained dialogues between schoolboard members or judges and potential censors. However, there have been more traditional essays among the best papers as well.

The follow-up benefits have also been encouraging. The discussions continue after the assignment has been graded and returned. Students often drop by with articles for my growing censorship file, and a few students have later pursued censorship topics for full-blown research projects. More importantly, another classroom of students has heard that teachers *do* select books carefully, and these students have done some serious thinking about the defense of challenged materials and the impact of censorship on education.

Jackie E. Swenson, Thornton High School, Thornton, Colorado

Travel in the U.S.A.

This research and writing project is one of the most productive I have used in past years. Students use various forms of written and oral communications, participate in independent research and group discussion, and learn, from the vantage point of a tourist, what is involved in planning and taking a trip to another state.

I give students a deadline several months ahead, allotting a few days in the beginning for reviewing and practicing writing business letters. To give students an overview of the project, I explain that "Travel in the U.S.A." will involve students in:

planning a two-week tour of a state

writing letters for information about a state

writing a thesis statement for a tour folder

preparing a workable budget for a trip

using a road atlas to plan and record travel routes

writing descriptively and imaginatively

obtaining information from resources such as magazines, tour guides, atlases, newspapers, and other travelers

I recommend to my students the following possible resources: *National Geographic, The Reader's Guide to Periodical Literature, Southern Living, Travel and Leisure,* road atlases, travel files in public libraries, travel agents, travel brochures and booklets provided by travel agencies, the travel section of major newspapers, state tourist bureaus, encyclopedias, and members of travel clubs or other people who have traveled extensively.

Students must complete much of the work outside class, following the list of required tasks on the handout sheet shown below. I go over each task on the list and answer questions before students begin work. For help in pursuing particular tasks, students may meet in small discussion groups in class at designated times throughout the project.

I periodically ask students to bring in their work for proofreading and editing in peer writing groups and for my comments and suggestions. At these checkpoints I can also help students who are getting behind or are in need of additional direction. After the projects are completed and the results are assembled in "travel folders," I set aside several class periods for the sharing of folders within and between classes.

I have used this project for four years, making minor changes each year. I hope that other teachers interested in combining research, writing, and practical knowledge will find this a useful approach.

Guidelines for a "Travel in the U.S.A." Project

1. In this project, you will plan and take an imaginary trip to another state. Select a state that you have not visited and would like to visit or one that you have visited but know little about.

2. To request information about travel and tourism, write a letter to the state's travel bureau in the capital city and to the chambers of commerce of any cities in which you are interested. Specifically, ask for information and literature on overnight accommodations, state and national parks, wildlife refuges, museums, historical sites, and other points of interest. (As you research your state and find references to specific places you might like to visit, jot down the names and addresses and write to request information.) Remember to keep for your travel folder a copy of any letters you write.

3. Take notes on your chosen state from *at least* five sources. Use at least two different encyclopedias, an atlas, one book, and one periodical. Copy the notes onto index cards, using one side only. State your source for each; include titles of books, articles, or chapters, publishers, dates of publication, and page numbers. You might want to research some of the following questions about your state:

   > What are the best-known towns or cities and what makes them notable?
   >
   > What are the state's major and minor industries?
   >
   > What are the bordering states?
   >
   > What are the best-known historical sites and the most popular recreational sites?
   >
   > What are the names and locations of well-known schools?
   >
   > What is the average temperature for each season?
   >
   > What are the names and occupations of several famous people from the state?

4. Write a thesis statement about one-half page in length, in which you explain your reasons for wanting to visit this state and what you plan to do on your trip. Include both educational

and recreational plans. This page will be the first page of your travel folder.

5. Write a one- to two-page paper on the geographical features of the state. Compare several areas within the state as to geography, temperature, precipitation, and other factors.

6. Write a detailed travel itinerary for your proposed trip, specifying dates, times, places, and activities.

7. Decide how you will get to and from your destination. If you choose to fly, call a travel agent and find out the cheapest round-trip fare, whether the flight is direct or includes a stopover or change of planes, and the times of departure and arrival. If you plan to take a bus or a train, you may be able to obtain your information from a travel agent or you may have to call the bus or train station. If you plan to travel by car, use the car's mileage per gallon, the distance, and current gas prices to figure out how much the trip will cost. Also determine how long it will take to reach your destination.

8. Prepare an accurate budget for your trip. Allow yourself $2,000 and plan to return home with *no more* than $50. Your transportation to and from your destination, whether plane, train, bus, or car, must come out of this $2,000. Remember to allow for such things as meals and snacks; tips in restaurants, airports; and hotels; car rentals; bus or taxi rides within cities; tickets for movies, plays, or other forms of entertainment; souvenirs; postage; telephone charges; emergencies; and so on.

9. Make a list of what you plan to pack, keeping in mind the expected weather and the kind of activities you have planned. If you plan to fly, find out the current height and weight restrictions for luggage and plan your packing accordingly.

10. Write a daily personal diary for the duration of your trip. Include anecdotes about your adventures, descriptions of what you enjoyed the most, and notes on what you would do differently next time.

11. Write a letter to a friend at home about an exciting event from your trip.

12. Write a letter to your parents, a relative, or a teacher describing a historical point of interest from your trip.

13. Prepare a picture scrapbook of your trip, using pictures cut out of travel brochures and magazines and photocopied from books. Write a caption for each picture.

14. Write a short story about someone you met on your trip. Describe the person in detail and write about one or more memorable incidents involving this person.

15. Write a paragraph or a poem about your trip, focusing on sights and sounds particular to the state you visited.

16. Draw or trace a map of the state, indicating the capital and the points of interest that you visited. Plot your route in red.

17. Collect your completed assignments together in a travel folder and prepare a table of contents.

Peggy Gray, Pleasant Grove High School, Texarkana, Texas

Using Cubing to Generate Ideas for Definition and Description

As the writing teacher at our high school, I am often asked to give presentations in various courses across the curriculum. My job is to help students improve their writing in all their classes, not just English. This spring, the science teachers asked me to talk to their classes about essay exam responses. Instead of writing fully developed paragraphs of definition or description, students were answering with single sentences or even single phrases. To help students generate material for an essay response, I decided to adapt Elizabeth Cowan's cubing technique described in her college textbook, *Writing* (Scott, Foresman, 1983).

An excellent device for prewriting, cubing works with almost every topic. Cowan directs the writer to imagine a cube that has six different messages on it. I made some changes in Cowan's original to suit the type of scientific description that our students needed to know more about, but this activity can be just as helpful in English class as in the science class. The general student directions for cubing are as follows:

Imagine a cube—think of it as a solid block. Now imagine that each side has something different written on it. These are the rules for *cubing*:

1.   Use all six sides of the cube.

2.   Jot down ideas in a word or phrase. You can use the margin of your test sheet.

3.   Move as quickly as you can around the cube. One side of the cube says: *Classify it.* (To what larger group or groups does it belong? How do you know? In what ways is it like the group?)

Another side says: *Describe it.* (Color? Shape? Size? Exact size? Exact measurements? Texture? Does it stay the same or change?)

A third side says: *Analyze it.* (What is it made of? How is it made or created? What are its parts?)

The fourth side says: *Differentiate it.* (What makes it special? How is it distinguishable from other things with which it might be confused? How does it contrast with other members of the same group?)

The fifth says: *Locate it.* (Where can we find it? Under what conditions would we find it?)

The sixth side says: *Use it.* (What does it do? What is it good for? Or what is it bad for?)

The presentation was scheduled for our large lecture hall. Students would be coming from different types of science classes and would have different ability levels. With their general cubing directions in hand, and my oral instructions, students would complete a writing activity based on cubing. But I still needed to decide on *what* they would be cubing; I needed a subject that would work for all students and would also be so memorable that it would become a mnemonic device, reminding them of how to use cubing principles in other situations. These are the oral instructions I finally came up with:

You will need at least two sheets of paper. You will be writing a paragraph-long essay response, using cubing as a means of generating material for the essay. Your work will be taken up at the end of the period, and you will need to listen carefully because all the directions will be given orally.

Pretend you're a mad scientist, maybe somewhere in Transylvania. You've just created a new life form in your laboratory. Now you must make a report of your great discovery to the world. No one has heard of your creature yet. It's some sort of animal—you decide what type it will be. It could be a mammal, reptile, amphibian, bird or fish, but it can be only one of these types—no combinations.

(At this point, I give students a minute or two for a quick decision, and remind them not to discuss their creatures with anyone else.)

Picture your creature in your mind. Make up a name for your creature or call it "the monster." Put its name at the top of your page.

Have the handout about cubing in front of you. Let's look at the creature from each one of these angles.

1. First, let's classify your creature. What type of animal is it? Write a sentence: "My monster is a ——————— (mammal, reptile, bird, amphibian, fish)." Now write a sentence or two telling how you know it's that type of animal. For example, how do you know if it's a mammal? If you want to, you can start with "It is clearly a ——————— because ———————"
    (I pause at appropriate points to let students write, but I don't linger long.)

2. Description comes next. Use your imagination. What do you see in your mind? Things to consider are color, shape, size, texture. Does the creature stay the same or does it change like a chameleon? Describe your creature in a sentence or two.

3. Analyze it. What parts does your creature have? Consider first what might be inside. Does your creature have a heart, lungs, brain, and so on? Are there special features about these parts? Then consider the outside. What appendages does it have? Head, arms, legs, hands, toes, gills, fins, tail? How many toes does it have? What type of skin does it have? Does it have eyes, hair? You can use this format if you want: "The creature has ———————, ———————, and ———————. Its internal organs are ———————, ———————, ———————."

4. Differentiate it. What makes your creature special? Unique? Different from the animals, other mammals? You can use this sentence starter: "The creature is unique because ————."

5. Locate it. What sort of habitat would be best for the creature? Where is this creature likely to be found? And why is this type of habitat necessary? You may use this sentence starter: "This creature is found in a habitat that is ————, ————, and ————."

6. Use it. What is the creature good for? For example, could you use it as a substitute for a watchdog? *Does* it have a use? Why or why not? Is it harmful? If so, to whom or what? How does it fit into the ecosystem? You could start your explanation, "This creature is useful in that it ————," or "This creature is harmful in that it ————."

What you've done so far is basically what you need to do when you're asked to define and describe. By using the cubing technique, you can develop an essay response no matter what the subject: a poem, a chair, a computer program, a protein, a rock, or the human heart.

After leading students through this activity, I showed them a more traditional example on a transparency: a definition and description of "virus," taken from an encyclopedia. We located together the points where the author had used the six "cubing" perspectives.

As a humorous finale, students exchanged papers and drew each other's monsters. To demonstrate the importance of accuracy in description, I include this caveat in my instructions: if it's not in the description, it can't be added to the drawing.

Patricia ten Broeke, Leander High School, Leander, Texas